MacBook Air 2025 (M4) User Guide

The Ultimate Tips & Tricks Manual with Simple Instructions and Pictures for Beginners & Advanced User's to Use and Operate MacBook Air

Douglas C. McNally

TABLE OF CONTENTS

INTRODUCTION

Apple released two models of the 2025 MacBook Air, both featuring the same design but with different display sizes. The larger model boasts a 15.3-inch screen, while the smaller model measures 13.6 inches.

Just like the previous version, both models feature black bezels surrounding the screen. They come with a black Magic Keyboard, but they don't include a touch bar; however, they have a big Force Touch trackpad for gesture movement (including tap and force click) and navigation. Additionally, the keyboard has backlit keys that illuminate it in a low-light environment for ease of use.

At the left side of the device, there are two Thunderbolt/USB-C ports and the MagSafe charging port. On the right, there's the 3.5mm headphone jack. The 13-inch models come with a four-speaker audio setup, while the 15-inch models feature a six-speaker audio setup system.

MagSafe 3

Thunderbolt / USB 4

3.5 mm headphone jack

There's a 12-megapixel front-facing camera for FaceTime calls, to shoot photos, and to record videos.

The Touch ID fingerprint sensor, located at the upper area of the keyboard, can replace a password to unlock your device or authenticate online purchases in Safari.

The device features True Tone, an effect that adjusts the screen's color temperature and brightness to blend in with the ambient light; this also helps to reduce eyestrain.

Apple's M4 processor powers the 2025 MacBook Air, earning it the moniker MacBook Air M4. This chip delivers improved performance for video processing, applications, and games.

Thanks to the M4 chip, the device supports Apple Intelligence, which allows you to utilize artificial intelligence tools such as ChatGPT, image generation through the Image Playground app, text generation, create Genmoji, use Clean Up to remove background objects, and lots more features that will be introduced in subsequent updates. This user guide covers how to navigate these features and many more.

CHAPTER 1

PARTS OF MACBOOK AIR

Here are the physical features of the MacBook Air 2025:

Thunderbolt/USB 4 ports: Use this to charge your PC, connect cable and transfer files, charge other devices like iPad or keyboard, etc. Additionally, you can connect another screen or projector through this port.

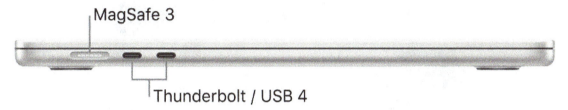

MagSafe 3 port: Connect the accompanying USB-C Power connecter to charge your MacBook battery. If the battery is running low, the indicator light will illuminate amber, and it turns to green when it's charged fully.

3.5mm headphone jack: You plug in your headphones or external speakers to this part to listen to audio or videos.

Touch ID: The power button is integrated into the Touch ID. You can tap it to power on your computer or simply raise the lid. You can also press the Touch ID button to lock your device. If you're starting up or restarting the device, you'll be required to sign in by typing your password. Also, you can utilize the Touch ID to confirm purchases rather than fill in your password.

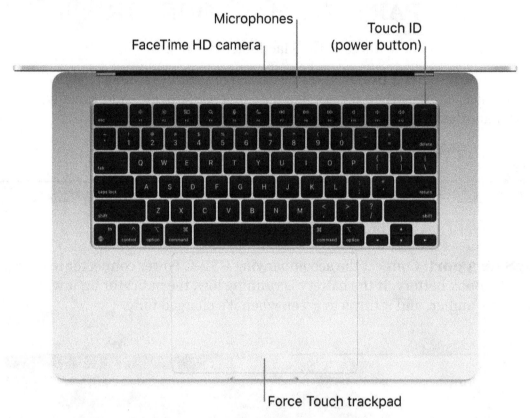

FaceTime HD camera: This is the MacBook camera. You can utilize this to capture photos and videos, as well as for FaceTime video calls. If the light glows, then camera is turned on.

Force Touch trackpad: Use this to navigate your computer and click anywhere on it to open a feature.

Speakers: The 15-inch model comprises of 6 speaker audio technology that has 2 tweeters as well as 2 pairs of force-canceling woofers, while the 13-inch model comprises of 4 speaker audio technology system with 2 tweeters and 2 woofers. The speakers integrates Spatial Audio

Microphones: Chat through audio and even record your voice through the inbuilt microphone.

MENU BAR

The menu bar is located at the top of the MacBook screen. You can press the menus and buttons to view status, select command and execute some tasks. You can also hide this bar so that it only appears when you drag the cursor to the screen's top.

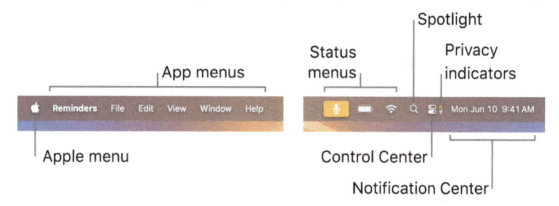

Apple menu

The Apple menu is situated at the upper left edge of the MacBook screen, from which you can access commonly used functions like app updates, System Settings, screen lock, and power off your device. Within the Apple menu, you'll find App Store, Shut Down, System Settings, and more.

App menus

Under the app menus which is positioned at the screen's top just next to the Apple menu, you'll find the Format, Help, View, Edit, or Window menu.

Status menus

The status menu contains icons such as battery, Wi-Fi, and microphone that let you view the status of your device.

Press the menu icon to view additional information about it. For instance, press the

Wi-Fi button to view the available networks or toggle on and off the Wi-Fi.

To reorganize the status menus, long-tap the Command key and drag a status menu icon simultaneously. Long-tap the Command key and at the same time slide the icon away from the menu bar to delete a status icon.

Spotlight

Press the Spotlight icon to search for documents, audio, movies, and apps on both your Mac and internet.

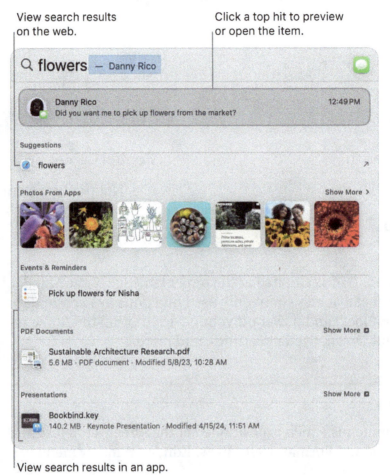

View search results on the web.

Click a top hit to preview or open the item.

View search results in an app.

Notification Center

When you press the date and time in the menu bar, it will take you to the Notification Center. Under the Notification Center, you can see widgets and see your missed alerts.

Control Center

Tapping the Control Center button will take you to the Control Center menu, wherein you'll find your most used features like Bluetooth, Sound, Focus, AirDrop and more.

When you see an orange dot 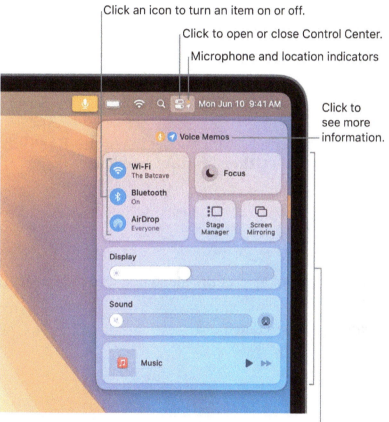 next to this menu, it shows that your microphone is been utilized; a purple dot shows that an audio recording is ongoing; and a green dot means that the camera is in use. If you see an arrow , it shows that your location is been used by your MacBook.

Click an icon to turn an item on or off.

Click to open or close Control Center.

Microphone and location indicators

Click to see more information.

For some controls, click to see more options.
For Stage Manager, click to turn it on or off.

Use Control Center

- Go to the menu bar, hit the Control Center button .

Perform any of the following actions:

- Use the trackpad to slide a slider to change a setting. For instance, slide the Sound slider upward or downward to change the Mac's volume.

- Press an icon to enable or disable it. For instance, press Wi-Fi or AirDrop to activate or deactivate it.
- Press a button to see additional options. For instance, press the Focus button to see your Focus list and enable or disable a Focus, or hit the Screen Mirroring button to select a target screen.

Customize Control Center

You can reorganize and manage the Control Center from the menu bar.

- Hit the Apple menu .
- Next, press **System Settings**.
- From the sidebar, hit the Control Center button . (Scroll downward if needed).
- Then select your preferred settings under the **Menu Bar Only**, **Control Center Modules**, and **Other Modules** sections.

Turn on Bluetooth

Press the Control Center icon at the menu bar, and then select the Bluetooth icon to activate your Mac's Bluetooth.

USE AIRDROP

Using AirDrop, you can easily transfer media files to another nearby Apple device.

For safety reasons, all transfers are protected with encryption and the receiver has the option to accept or reject each one individually.

Keep in mind that once an AirDrop has begun, it stays running over the internet even if you're outside the Bluetooth or Wi-Fi zone.

Before starting, ensure that Wi-Fi and Bluetooth are enabled on both gadgets.

Also, ensure that the sending and receiving devices are not more than thirty feet from each other.

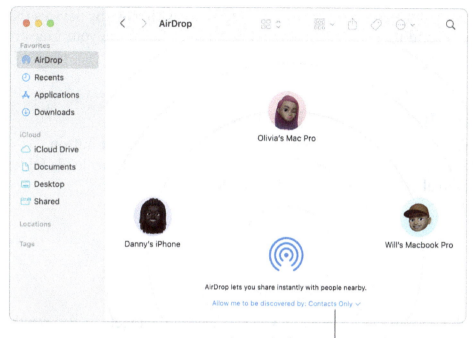

Control who can
send items to you.

Turn on AirDrop

- Select the Control Center icon at the menu bar, and then hit the
  AirDrop button . If it becomes blue, it means it is turned on.

- To select the people that can transfer files to you, press the arrow icon
  next to **AirDrop**, then press the **Everyone** or **Contacts Only** option.

Sending an item with AirDrop

In order to utilize AirDrop to transfer files to someone, ensure that the person
receiving the file have activated AirDrop and also opted to receive files from
Everyone or Contacts.

If they choose the later, ensure your information is saved in their contacts list.

- Navigate to the item you wish to share.

- Select the Share icon at the toolbar.
- Next, tap **AirDrop**.

- Choose the person you would want to share with. Nearby devices that are Wi-Fi and Bluetooth enabled and can receive files from your Mac are the ones you see on the dialog menu.

Receive items with AirDrop
- When you see the AirDrop notification, tap the **Accept** button.
- Certain files will automatically be stored under the Downloads folder. You could also be able to select a location to store them.

NOTIFICATION CENTER

You can see your missed alerts, and you can even add widgets to also see things like the weather, upcoming meetings, birthdays, and trending news in the Notification Center.

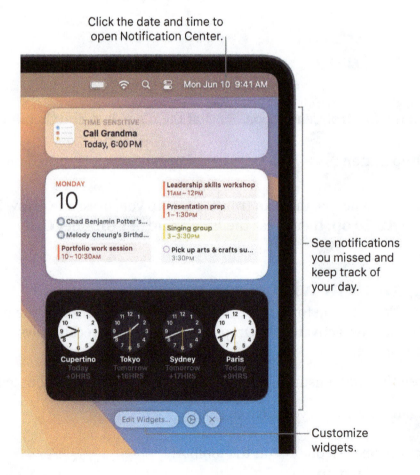

Open or Exit the Notification Center

To access the Notification Center, move your cursor to the menu bar, then press the date and time. Otherwise, use your two fingers to slide left from the right corner of your trackpad.

To exit the Notification Center, click the date and time once more, or tap somewhere on the desktop, utilize your two fingers to slide right to the right corner of the Mac's trackpad.

Use notifications in Notification Center

Drag your cursor across an alert that appears in the Notification Center, and then perform any of these tasks:

- **Enlarge or collapse a group of notifications**: If the alerts from an application are grouped, then several alerts are stacked. Tap anyplace in the notification's top to enlarge and view all the alerts. Press the "**Show less**" button to collapse the stack.
- **Perform an action**: Press the action. Let's say you got an alert from the Calendar app, you can hit the **Snooze** button on the notification. If you got an email, you can press the **Reply** button on the notification.

- When you see the arrow icon ∨ next to an action, it means they have more options, click the arrow to view it.
- **View additional information**: Tap the alert to access the item within the

  application. If the app's name is accompanied by an arrow ❯ , you can get further details by clicking on the arrow.
- **Tweak an app's alert settings**: If you see an arrow appears on the right

  of the app's name, then press the arrow ❯ , hit the More icon ••• , and silent, disable alert, or select **Notification Settings** to adjust them.

- Clear notifications: To clear a single notification, press the Clear icon ⊗ .

  To clear all, drag your cursor across the Clear icon ⊗ on the upper notification on the stack, and then choose **Clear All**.

USE THE DOCK ON MAC

The Dock is always positioned on the MacBook's desktop. You can find frequently used applications and functions, including Launchpad, Settings, App Store, and the Trash. The dock appears at the bottom of the screen by default, but you can move it left or right.

Apps | Trash

Downloads folder

Open items in the Dock

Here are something's, you can do on the Dock:

- Launch an app: Tap the application button. For instance, to launch the Finder, tap its icon 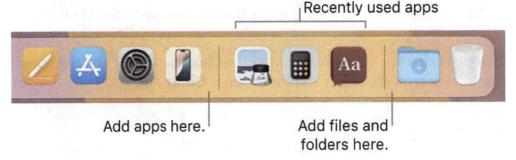 in the Dock.
- **View a file in an application**: Use the cursor to move the file across the application's icon. For instance, to view a Pages document, move the file on top of the Pages icon that's located in the Dock.
- **Display a content in the Finder**: Command-tap the content's icon.
- **Hide the current application and return to the previous one**: Simply, Option-tap the current application's icon.
- **Hide other applications and move to another one**: Option-Command-tap the application icon that you wish to go to.
- **Force quit an application**: If you're using an application and it freezes, Control-click the application's icon, and then hit **Force Quit.**

Adding, removing, & rearranging Dock items

Recently used apps

Add apps here. | Add files and folders here.

12

- **Adding an item to the Dock**: Use the cursor to move applications to the left (or on top) the strip that divides the recently used applications. Slide the folders and files towards the right side of (or under) the other strip separating the recently used applications.
- **Removing an icon from the Dock**: Use the cursor to tap and slide the icon away from the Dock until the **Remove** button appears. The item will still be in your Mac, but will no longer show in the Dock. If you mistakenly accidentally deleted it from the Dock, you can restore. Navigate to open the app; its icon will now show on the Dock. Then, Control-tap the application's icon, and then press **Options**, then choose **Keep in Dock**.
- **Reorganize items**: use the cursor to move the items to another position.

Customize the Dock

- On the MacBook, press the Apple menu  under the menu bar.
- Next, select **System Settings**.
- Here, press the **Desktop & Dock** button on the sidebar.
- Under the **Dock** section, adjust the settings you like.

CONNECT YOUR MAC TO A WI-FI

When attempting to connect to a Wi-Fi network, ensure the Wi-Fi is powered on and that you're within range of the network. If the Wi-Fi network is encrypted, ensure you have the password handy.

Join a public Wi-Fi network
- Go over to the menu bar on the MacBook, then press the Wi-Fi button

- Select the network you wish to join. If it's not visible, hit **Other Networks** to show available networks
- If prompted, fill in the network's password, and then press **Join**.

Join a hidden Wi-Fi network

If you're connecting to a hidden network, you must have gotten its name, password, and security type handy since they don't publicly show their name.

- Go to the menu bar, then press the Wi-Fi icon .
- Next, choose the Other Networks option.
- Under the Other Networks list, hit the **Other** button.
- Type the network's name inside the Network Name box.
- Next, press the Security pop-up menu.
- Select the security protocol of the network.
- Fill in other required information, then hit **Join**.

CHAPTER 2

CREATE AN APPLE ACCOUNT

With an Apple account, you can explore and use plethoras of Apple services such as iCloud, the App Store, FaceTime, and several more. To log in, you'll need to provide an email address (e.g., yourname@icloud.com) and then the associated password of the Apple account.

You can utilize your existing email address to set up an Apple account or sign up for a free iCloud email.

Some regions will require you to enter a phone number rather than an email address when attempting to set up an Apple account.

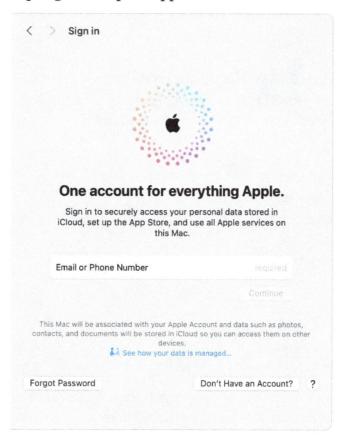

- On the Mac, press the Apple menu on the menu bar.
- Next, choose **System Settings**.
- From the sidebar's top, tap "**Sign in**".
- Here, press the **Don't Have an Account?** button.
- Follow the onscreen directions.

Sign in to your Apple Account

If you already created an Apple account, then do this to log in:

- On the Mac, press the Apple menu  on the menu bar.
- Here, press **System Settings**.
- At the sidebar's top, select "**Sign in**". You are already logged in if your name shows up.
- Type in the email address or phone number associated with your Apple Account.
- Click **Continue**.
- Fill in your password, then hit **Continue**.
- Follow the onscreen prompts.

Sign out of your Apple Account

If you're giving away your Mac, you should make sure to log out of your Apple Account so the recipient don't have access to your data.

- Select the Apple menu from the menu bar.
- Then choose **System Settings**.
- Tap your name at the sidebar's top.
- Then hit **Sign Out**.
- Follow the onscreen directions to complete.

Set up iCloud

iCloud ensures that your data is safe, always updated, and accessible from any device you own. You can easily share media with loved ones, whether it's images, documents, notes, or anything else, all through iCloud.

You'll have to choose the iCloud services to utilize after logging into your Apple Account.

Upgrade iCloud storage or view details.

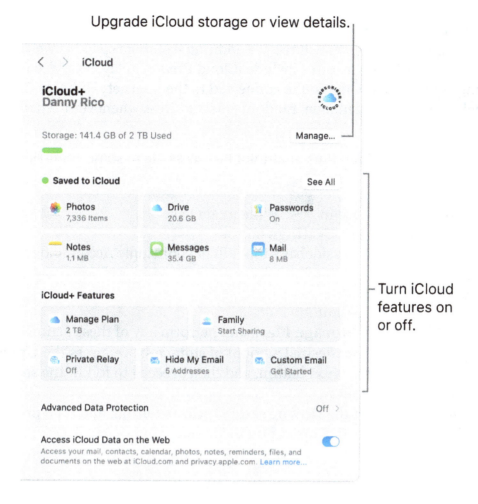

Turn iCloud features on or off.

Enable iCloud

1. On the Mac, press the Apple menu on the menu bar.
2. Here, press **System Settings**.
3. At the sidebar's top, tap your name. If your name isn't showing, press "**Sign in**," and fill in your Apple Account sign in details.
4. Next, tap **iCloud**.
5. Choose from the following options (to view all, choose **See All**):
- Choose an iCloud service such as **Mail** or **iCloud Drive**, and toggle the switch for "**Sync this Mac**".
- If the "**Sync this Mac**" doesn't appear, press the **Turn On** or **Turn Off** button.
- Toggle the switch next to iCloud services like **Reminders** or **Calendars**.

Upgrade to iCloud+

By upgrading to iCloud+, you will receive additional storage space as well as premium services. These features include iCloud Private Relay, a service for protecting your privacy while you're connected to the internet; Hide My Email, which helps to generate a unique, random email address whenever needed; and several others.

Please be aware that iCloud Plus might not be accessible in some countries.

1. Choose the Apple menu ![Apple icon] at the menu bar.
2. Then hit the **System Settings** button.
3. Tap your name at the sidebar's top. Fill in your Apple Account log in information.
4. Next, tap **iCloud**.
5. Select the **Manage** button.
6. Then hit **Change Storage Plan**, and perform any of these actions:
- Upgrade: Select your desired amount of storage space, press the **Upgrade to iCloud+**, or the **Next** button, and then proceed to follow the steps that appear on the monitor.
- Downgrade: Select the **Downgrade Options** button, and then proceed to follow the prompts that appear on the monitor.

Enable iCloud Photos

- Hit the Apple menu ![Apple icon] at the menu bar.
- Next, choose the **System Settings** button.
- Press your name at the sidebar's top. Type your Apple Account log in credentials, if asked.
- Then, press **iCloud**.
- Next, tap **Photos**.
- Toggle on "**Sync this Mac**."

Use Touch ID on Mac

You can unlock your MacBook, make payment in the App Store, as well as utilize Apple Pay for online transactions, with Touch ID that's embedded into your Mac or Magic Keyboard. Touch ID can additionally be used to log into third-party applications.

Upgrade iCloud storage or view details.

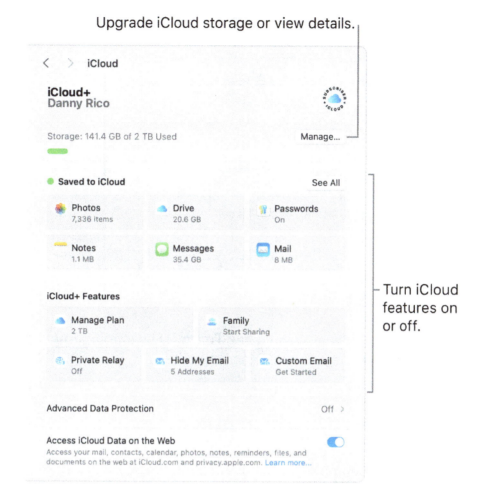

Turn iCloud
features on
or off.

Set up Touch ID

- Press the Apple menu 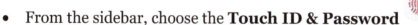 at the menu bar.
- Next, choose **System Settings**.

- From the sidebar, choose the **Touch ID & Password** button.
- Then, press **Add Fingerprint**.
- Fill in your password, and then follow the prompts.
- You can find the Touch ID sensor at the upper right corner of the Mac's keyboard. You'll be able to add 3 fingerprints to a user account.

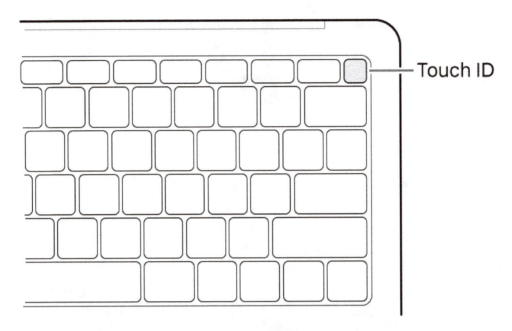

Touch ID

- Select your preferred method of using Touch ID by tapping Apple Pay, Autofill passwords, Unlock your Mac, and others.

Rename or remove fingerprints

- Select the Apple menu at the menu bar.
- Next, press **System Settings**.

- From the sidebar, choose the **Touch ID & Password** button.

  Perform any of these actions:

- **Rename a fingerprint**: Press the text underneath a fingerprint, and then provide a name.
- **Delete a fingerprint**: Use the cursor and tap a fingerprint, type in your password, and choose **Unlock**, finally press **Delete**.

Utilize Touch ID to unlock, log in, or change users

Some tasks require that you use Touch ID before perform them.

- **To unlock your MacBook and password encrypted files**: Wake the MacBook, or navigate to the password encrypted file, then position your finger on the Touch ID when prompted.
- **Sign in from the log in menu**: To access your account, select your name from the sign in menu, then position your finger on the Touch ID.

- Touch ID can only be used to unlock password encrypted accounts. Touch ID cannot be used by users who are only allowed to share or by guests.

- **Change users**: Press the User button ⊙ from the menu bar, select another user, and then put your finger on the Touch ID key.

Change the login password

Best security practices entails changing your login password periodically.

Keep in mind that anytime you power on or wake up the MacBook from sleep, you'll be prompted to fill in your login password. Your login password is different from your Apple Account password.

- Hit the Apple menu .
- Next, choose **System Settings**.
- Next, select **Users & Groups** .

- Tap the Info icon ⓘ that is situated next to your username.
- Then select **Change**.
- Fill in your present password into the **Old Password** column.
- Type in the new password you wish to use into the **New Password** column, and then confirm by entering it once more into the **Verify** column.
- Please provide a suggestion to assist you in remembering the password. When you repeat an incorrect password three times or when you hit the question mark next to the password column on the login menu, the hint will be displayed.
- Tap the "**Change Password**" option.

Add a user or group

Make sure to create separate accounts for each user on your computer; this way, everyone may make their own adjustments to the system preferences without impacting anybody else. Allowing infrequent users to sign in as guests ensures that they cannot access the data or settings of other users.

- Select the Apple menu ![Apple logo] at the menu bar.
- Next, choose **System Settings**.
- Here, select the **Users & Groups** option from the sidebar.

- Then press the Add User button ![Add User icon] underneath the list of users. (You'd be required to type in your password.)
- Tap the dialog window next to **New User**, and then select the type of user: Administrator, Sharing Only, or Standard.

- To know more about each type of user, press the Help icon (?) at the bottom -left edge of the pop-up.
- Provide the full name of the new user. The account name will be created automatically. To modify the generated name, type in your preferred name.
- Type in the user's password, then confirm it. Provide a hint to assist the user in remembering their password.
- Next, tap the "**Create User**" button.

Update your login photo

You can modify the background image that shows up in the sign in screen. The sign in photo is also the profile photo of your Apple account, and it appears on your My Card in Contacts.

You will not be able to tweak the profile image of another person who is currently signed in (shown with a checkbox next to their photo) unless they do it themself or they sign our so you can modify it.

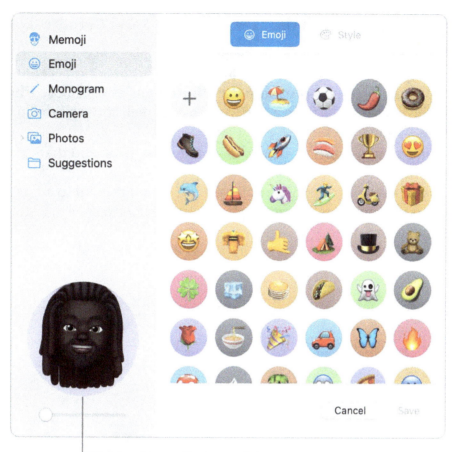

Click to change the user picture.

1. Hit the Apple menu 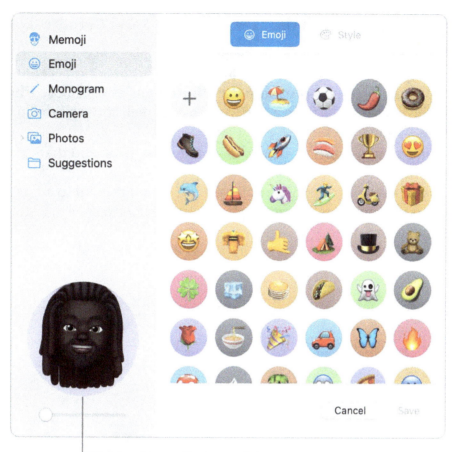 at the menu bar.
2. Next, tap **System Settings**.

3. Then select **Users & Groups** 👥 .
4. Select the photograph next to your sign in name, and then perform one of these tasks:

- **Choose a Memoji**: Select **Memoji**, then press the Add icon ⊕ to choose and create a facial photo. Alternatively, choose one of the Memoji that appears, and then choose a posture and appearance that you prefer.

- **Choose an emoji**: Select **Emoji**, and then press the Add icon ⊕ to choose a photograph under the emoji gallery. Alternatively, choose any of the emoji that appears, and choose a style.
- **Choose a monogram**: Tap **Monogram**, click a background color, and then type in your initials.

- **Capture a photo with the Mac's camera**: Select **Camera**. Position your shot, and then select the Camera icon 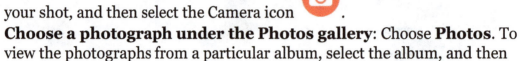 .
- **Choose a photograph under the Photos gallery**: Choose **Photos**. To view the photographs from a particular album, select the album, and then choose a photograph.
- **Choose a suggested photo**: Choose **Suggestions**, and then click the photograph.
5. Once you've chosen a photograph, you can drag it around to adjust the location or move the slider either way to zoom in or out.
6. Finally, press **Save**.

CHAPTER 3

OPEN APPS ON MAC

On the MacBook, you can keep many applications open at once. This works particularly well for applications like Safari and Mail that you use often.

Clicking an application's icon in the Dock is the fastest method to launch it on a Mac.

Click an app icon
to open the app.

There are several methods to launch the application on a Mac in case its icon is not in the Dock:

- From the Dock, select the Launchpad button 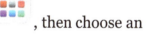, then choose an application icon.

Click to open an app.

Drag an app over another
to create a folder.

Click the dots or swipe
to see more apps.

- Open an app with the help of Siri . Just say, "Open Calculator."

- Select Spotlight button from the main menu, type the name of an app into the search bar, and then hit **Return**.

- To access apps that you have recently used, go to the Apple menu , select **Recent Items**, and then select an application.

- Press the Finder icon from the Dock, then tap on **Applications** under the sidebar menu, and then double-tap the app.

Find and open apps in Launchpad

- Select the Launchpad app from the Dock.
- Enter the application's name that you are searching for in the search box at the Launchpad's top menu.
- Then tap the application to open it.

Remove apps from Launchpad

- Select the Launchpad application from the Dock.
- Long-tap the application until all the applications starts to shake.

- Then select the app's Delete icon .

  The Delete icon will not appear if the application cannot be deleted from Launchpad.

MOVE & ARRANGE APP WINDOWS ON MAC

A new window appears on the desktop whenever you launch an app or launch the Finder on a Mac. At any one moment, the menu bar will display the name of the currently active app (in bold) along with its associated menus.

Applications like Safari and Mail allow you to launch several windows or various kinds of windows simultaneously. You have many options for managing open application windows and closing them individually or all the window at once.

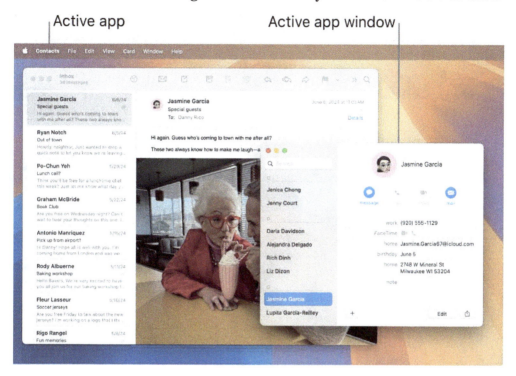

Move, align, & merge app windows

Perform any of these actions:

- **Manually drag a window**: To reposition the window, simply drag the window's title bar. Certain windows are immovable.

- **Position a window to one side on your desktop**: Press the cursor across the green icon at the upper left edge of the menu, select the icon on either the left or right side of the screen beneath the **Move & Resize** option. You can choose which half of the display the window occupies; the Dock and menu bar will still be showing.

- **Reposition a window to the screen's top or bottom**: To move the window, hover your mouse over the green icon at the upper left edge and click either the top or bottom button that appears underneath **Move & Resize**. You can still see the Dock and menu bar even when the window takes up half of the top or bottom screen.

27

- **Align windows**: You may align windows by dragging them close to each other; as they get closer, they will come into alignment without overlapping. It is possible to place many windows side by side.
- To ensure windows next to each other are equal in size, drag the corner you wish to resize, then once it gets closer to the next window, it'll automatically aligns with the corners.

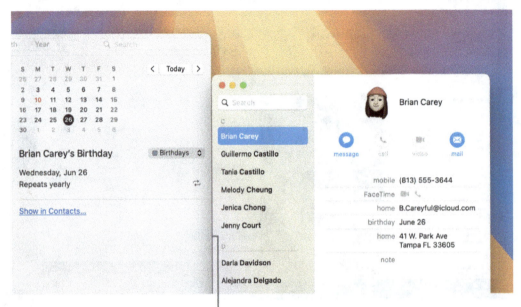

Drag the edge until it stops, aligned with the edge of the adjacent window.

- **Combine an application's windows into a single tabbed window**: Head to the app's menu and select **Window**, then choose **Merge All Windows**. Apps that have several window types (like Mail, which has both a viewer window as well as a new message window) will only merge the open window.
- In order to make a tab into a different window once more, choose the tab, then tap the **Window** menu, and then select **Move Tab to New Window**. Alternatively, you can simply move the tab away from the window.

Maximize or minimize app windows

- Make the window bigger: Place the mouse cursor on the green icon at the upper -left edge of the application window, and tap the Fill button underneath **Fill & Arrange**, or just hit the **Fn-Control-F** keys. To go back to the former window's size, Option-click the icon once more.

- **Make a window smaller**: Select the yellow minimize icon at the window upper -left edge, or hit the Command-M keys.

Quickly switch between app windows

- **Return to the previous application**: Hit the Command-Tab keys.
- **Go through all the open applications**: Long-tap the Command key on the keyboard, hit the Tab key, and then hit the Right or Left arrow key until you're in the application you prefer, then let go of the Command key.
- If you no longer wish to switch applications by scrolling across them, hit the Esc or the Period key, and then let go of the Command key.

Close one or all windows for an app

- **Exit one window**: While in the window, select the Close icon at the upper-left edge of the window. Alternatively, hit the Command-W keys.
- **Exit all opened windows for an application**: Hit the Option-Command-W keys.
- Even if you close all of an app's windows, it will still be open (you can tell its open by the little dot beneath its Dock icon). Hit the Command-Q keys to quit the application. Go to the Quit applications category.
- The Command-H keys allows you to hide the currently open application.

USE APPS IN FULL SCREEN

Most of the applications allows you to work in full-screen mode to eliminate distractions.

1. Choose any of these to enter full-screen:

- Tap the green icon at the upper-left edge of the window.
- Place your mouse cursor on the green icon at the window's upper-left edge, select **Full Screen**, and then tap the **Entire Screen** button.

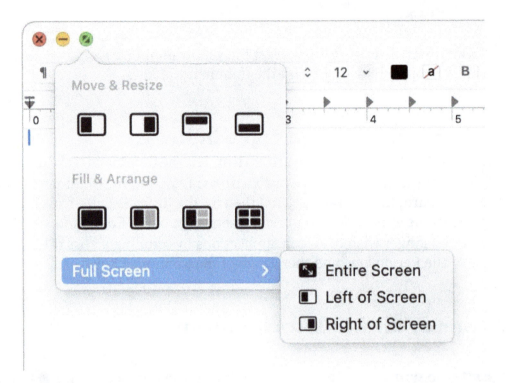

2. While the window is in full screen, perform one of these tasks:

- If you want the menu bar to be shown or hidden while in full-screen, place the Mac's cursor at the top or outside the screen's top.
- If you want the Dock to be shown or hidden while in full-screen, place the Mac's cursor at the Dock's location or out of it.
- To switch between other applications in full screen, swipe right or left on the trackpad using your three fingers.
- To exit the application full screen, place the cursor on the green icon once more, you'll see some options, hit the **Exit Full Screen** button.

USE APPS IN SPLIT VIEW

Most of the applications allows you to utilize Split View on the MacBook; a feature which lets you simultaneously work on two open applications next to each other.

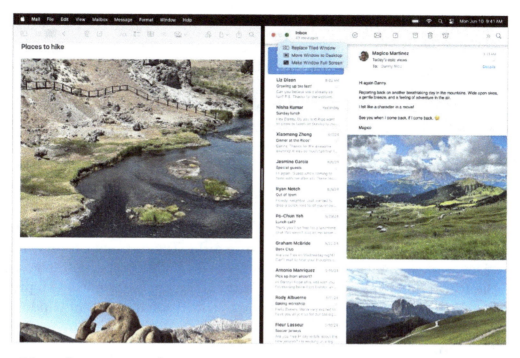

1. Move the cursor to the green icon at the upper-left edge of the window, click **Full Screen**, and then select the **Left of Screen** or **Right of Screen** button.

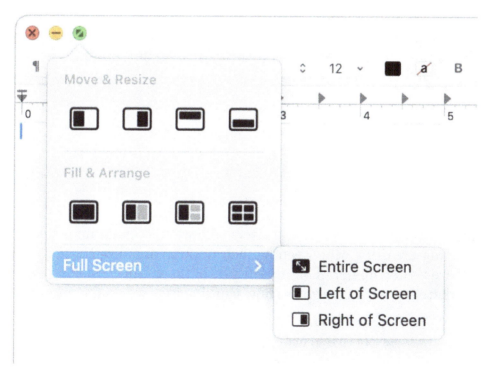

2. From the other section of the display, tap the second application you wish to open. At this moment, the Split View will be created.
3. Perform one of these tasks while in Split View:

- **Reveal or hide the menu bar**: Just drag the cursor to the top or outside of the screen's top.
- **Reveal or hide the Dock**: Place the cursor on the Dock's location or away from it.
- **Reveal or hide window's name & toolbar**: Tap the window, place the Mac's cursor at the screen's top or away from it.
- **Expand one part of the screen**: Place the Mac's cursor on the dividing bar positioned in the center, then slide it right or left. To go back to the default size, click two times on the dividing bar.
- **Switch sides**: Place the cursor on the window's name and toolbar, then slide it to the opposite side.
- **Utilize another application on one side**: Tap the application window, place your computer's cursor on the green icon at the upper-left edge, select the **Replace Tiled Window** option, and then tap the window you prefer to use. If along the line, you don't intend to substitute the current window, tap the desktop to go back to it.
- **Drag an application window to desktop**: Tap the application window, place the Mac's cursor on the green icon at the window's upper -left edge, then hit the **Move Window to Desktop** button. You'll see that the application will appear on the desktop.
- **Utilize an application window in full-screen**: Tap the application window, place the Mac's cursor on the green icon at the window's upper -left edge, and then hit the **Make Window Full Screen** option.

ORGANIZE THE DESKTOP WITH STAGE MANAGER

Stage Manager is a useful tool for Mac users who want to maintain focus on the application they are using while keeping their desktop organized. The apps you've used lately are neatly organized on the left side of the monitor, making them easy to access, whereas the window you're now working in takes up the middle part of your monitor's.

You can put windows where you want them, resize them, and even overlap them if you like. Using Stage Manager, you can also organize numerous applications on the screen so they collaborate. Each app in a group will launch in the screen's center when you move to that group.

Turn Stage Manager on or off

Stage Manager and regular windows are easily switchable, so you may use whichever one is most appropriate for the task at hand.

Pick an option here to use your Mac:

- Select the Apple icon ![Apple] from the menu bar, then press **System Settings**. Next, hit the **Desktop & Dock** ![icon] option that's under the sidebar. Navigate to the **Desktop & Stage Manager** section, and then toggle on or off **Stage Manager**.

- Press the Control Center icon ![toggle] at the menu bar, and hit the **Stage Manager** button ![button] to toggle it on or off.

If you're unable to enable Stage Manager, then hit the Apple menu ![Apple], and choose **System Settings**, then select **Desktop & Dock.** Here, navigate to **Mission Control**, toggle on "**Displays have separate Spaces.**"

Use Stage Manager

Perform one of these actions on your Mac:

- **Switch applications**: Select an application from the list on the left.
- **Organize the windows**: Customize your workflow by resizing, moving, and overlapping windows.
- **Group applications**: Select one app on the left and drop it into a cluster of applications in the middle.
- **Ungroup applications**: In order to remove an application from the group, just drag it to the left part of the monitor.

  There won't be a list of applications on the left side of Stage Manager if you disabled "**Show recent apps in Stage Manager**" in the settings. To display it, go to the left side of the screen and drag the cursor there.

Show or hide Stage Manager in the menu bar

You will find the Stage Manager in the Control Center at all times. Additionally, you can make it also appear on the menu bar.

- Select the Apple icon ![apple icon] from the menu bar.
- Next, hit the **System Settings** button.

- Next, hit the Control Center button ![control center icon] .
- Hit the dialog menu that is to the Stage Manager option.
- Finally, press the **Don't Show in Menu Bar** or **Show in Menu Bar** option.

Change Stage Manager settings

1. Hit the Apple menu ![apple icon] .
2. Next, choose **System Settings**.

3. Here, select the **Desktop & Dock** button.
4. Navigate to the **Desktop & Stage Manager** section.
5. Tick or unselect the checkboxes that appears next to **Show Items**:
- **On Desktop**: To display desktop items.
- **In Stage Manager**: To display desktop items anytime Stage Manager is activated.

Once this option is disabled, everything on the desktop will become hidden; to reveal them, just tap on the desktop.

6. Hit the "**Click wallpaper to reveal desktop**" dialog menu, and then select an option:

- **Only in Stage Manager**: Anytime you enable Stage Manager, once you tap the wallpaper, it will move aside all the windows and will make the desktop content including the widgets visible.
- **Always**: If you choose this option, when you tap the wallpaper, it will move every windows away and display the desktop items including the widgets.

7. Toggle on or off the **Stage Manager** option.
8. Toggle on or off the "**Show recent apps in Stage Manager**" option.

If you disable this option, your recently used applications will not be visible hidden, but you can place your cursor on the left corner of the monitor to briefly make them appear.

9. Hit the "**Show windows from an application**" drop-down menu, and then pick an option:

- **All at Once**: Display every available windows for an application anytime you navigate to it.
- **One at a Time**: Display just the most recently opened window for the application anytime you navigate to it.

If this option is disabled, and you need to go to another window, just tap the application in the left once more to access the next window that is available.

USE THE APP STORE

Use the search bar or categories in the App Store to locate an application you wish to install. Once you discover something you like, you can download or buy it using your Apple Account, or redeem a code.

Browse these areas for apps.

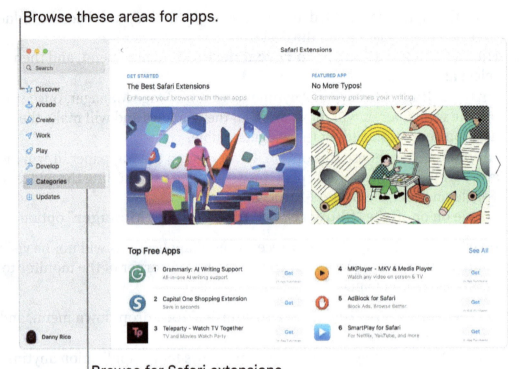

Browse for Safari extensions.

Find and buy apps

- On your MacBook, open the App Store .
- To search for applications, type in the words into the search box at the upper-left edge of the App Store, and then hit the Return key.
- Also, you can tap **Create**, **Categories**, **Discover** to find more apps.
- Tap an application's name or button to read its description and other information.

Review how an app developer handles your data.

Data Not Collected

The developer does not collect any data from this app.

- Tap the "**Get**" or price button to start downloading the application. Press the button once more to install or purchase the application.

Pause a download

When downloading an application, you can pause it, and resume at a later time.

- To pause the download, press the Pause button .
- To resume the download after pausing it, hit the Resume button  .

Cancel a download

- Select the Finder button  from the Dock menu.
- Navigate to the Applications folder, and then Control-click the application button.
- Finally, hit **Move to Trash**.

Adjust settings for downloads & purchases

1. Hit the Apple menu .
2. Next, choose **System Settings**.
- Select your name from the sidebar's top. If your name is not showing, select "**Sign in with your Apple Account**."
- Then press **Media & Purchases**.
- Finally, select your options.

Uninstall apps

- Choose the Launchpad button  from the Dock menu.
- Tap and press the app.

- Finally, hit the Cancel button .

Reinstall apps

You can still reinstall an application that you bought or freely downloaded using your Apple Account even if you uninstalled or removed it.

- On the Mac, launch the App Store .
- If you aren't already logged in, select **Sign In**; otherwise, select your name at the lower left edge.
- Find the application that you wish to reinstall, and hit the Download button .

CREATE A PASSWORD USING PASSWORD APP

The Password app holds all of your security credentials such as codes, passwords, and passkeys. In the app, you can create a password that you can utilize for websites and applications.

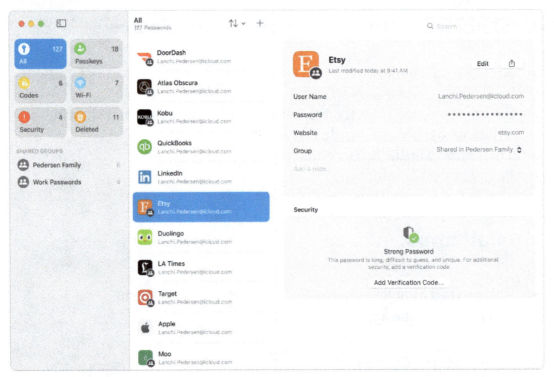

- Select the Passwords app .
- From the sidebar, select **All**.

- Then select the plus button ╋ .
- Fill in the website or application information, including the account's username.
- Next, press the **Password** column, and select an option of either **Strong Password** or **Without Special Characters**.
- Finally, tap **Save**.

Search the internet using Safari

You can visit websites or search through the search engines to find content on the internet.

- Select the Safari app on the Mac.
- Type in a word into the search column.
- Safari will show some suggestions as you type.
- Then select one of the suggestion, or hit the Return key to search with your chosen search engine.
- Clicking on a suggestion either loads the suggested page or opens an interactive window with helpful details.

Clear your browsing history in Safari on Mac

You can erase any traces of your web browsing history from Safari by deleting your browsing records.

- Select the Safari app on the Mac.
- Then select **History**.
- Here, press **Clear History**.
- Tap the dialog menu.
- Select a time range for when you want the history erased.

SELECT ITEMS

You can choose one or multiple items (folders, images, contacts, files) by performing any of these actions:

- **Choose an item**: Place the cursor on the item, and then tap it.
- **Choose more than one item**: Hold down the Command key, then tap the items.
- **Choose multiple items that are placed side by side**: Tap the first item to choose it, hold down the Shift key, and then tap the last item.
  Or, you can tap close to the first item, long-tap the trackpad, and then drag across all the items.

USE SIRI

Siri comes built-in into the MacBook. It is an intelligent assistant that can help you with everyday tasks like making a reminder, scheduling a meeting, or summarizing an article.

Turn on Siri

- Press the Apple menu 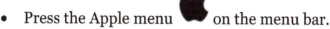 on the menu bar.
- Next, select **System Settings**.
- Here, choose **Apple Intelligence & Siri**.
- Toggle on Siri in case it isn't activated already, and then choose **Enable**.
- You'll be asked to enable Siri if you attempt to activate it when the option is not chosen. Ensure you have internet connection to utilize Siri.

When prompted, choose one of these options to help Siri and Dictation:

- Share audio recordings: Select the **Share Audio Recordings** to enable Apple to save audio of your device conversations with Siri.
- Keep audio recordings private: Press the "**Not Now**" button.

Activate Siri

Ensure you have internet connection to utilize Siri.

1. Perform any of these actions to activate Siri:

- Long-tap the Microphone key 🎤 on your Mac's keyboard.

- Hit the Siri 🔵 or Apple Intelligence Siri 🟣 under the menu bar.
- Just say "Siri" or "Hey Siri" (if you have this feature enabled n Siri settings).
2. Ask Siri anything - Just say something like, "set an alarm for 7am?" or "what's the result of last night's game?"

Turn off Siri

- Hit the Apple menu on the menu bar.
- Then press **System Settings**.

- Next, hit the **Apple Intelligence & Siri** button 🟣 .
- Then Toggle off **Siri**.

Add Siri to the menu bar

For ease of access, you can add the Siri control button to the menu bar.

- On the Mac, press the Apple menu 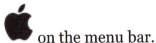 on the menu bar.
- Next, choose **System Settings**.

- Under the sidebar, press the Control Center .
- Navigate to **Menu Bar Only** (you'd have to scroll downward), press the pop-up menu that's next to Siri, and then pick an option.

Activate "Hey Siri" or "Siri" on Mac

Saying the word "Siri" or "Hey Siri" will activate Siri on your Mac. However, you'll need to ensure that it is enabled.

- On the MacBook, select the Apple menu on the menu bar.
- Next, choose **System Settings**.

- Here, press the **Apple Intelligence & Siri** button under the sidebar.
- Toggle on the "**Listen for**" button or select the word you wish to say to begin using Siri.
- Having this option enabled and the "**Allow Siri when locked**" toggled on; you'll be allowed to utilize Siri regardless of whether your Mac is in sleep mode or not.
- If you want to complete configuring "**Hey Siri**" or "**Siri**," just continue following the onscreen prompts.

Add a keyboard shortcut to activate Siri

- On the MacBook, press the Apple menu under the menu bar.
- Then hit **System Settings**.

- Next, hit the **Apple Intelligence & Siri** button under the sidebar.
- Press the pop-up menu that is next to the "**Keyboard shortcut**" section, and then pick a shortcut that will toggle on Siri or make yours.

Set the language and voice of Siri

- On the MacBook, press the Apple menu  under the menu bar.
- Then choose **System Settings**.

- Here, select the **Apple Intelligence & Siri** button  under the sidebar.
- Then select the pop-up menu that is next to **Language**.
- Select your preferred language.
- Then press the **Select** button that is next to **Voice** option, and then choose **Variations** or **Voices** from the pop-up menu that you see.

CHAPTER 4

CREATE & WORK WITH DOCUMENTS

You can create charts, reports, slideshows, spreadsheets, and others using some applications like TextEdit and Pages.

Create documents

1. Navigate to the application where you wish to create a document. For instance, go to TextEdit to make a text or HTML document.
2. From the Open menu, select **New Document**. Alternatively, select **File > New**.
3. Your device features some Apple applications for creating slideshows, reports, spreadsheets, and other types of files:
- **Pages**: You can create brochures, reports, banners, letters and other file types. In Pages you'll also get various built-in templates to quickly and easily design professional-looking documents.

- **Numbers**: Make use of spreadsheets to display and arrange your data. You can add math equations, charts, photos, and more to a already existing templates and then customize it to your liking.
- **Keynote**: Make presentations that stand out by adding media, graphs, motion pictures to slides, and more.

If these apps are not in your Mac, then you can install them from the App Store.

Format documents

When working on documents, you'll get multiple methods to format and edit your work.

- **Adjust the fonts & styles**: While working on the document, tap the **Format** button, then choose **Show Fonts**, select **Format**, click **Font**, and finally hit **Show Fonts**. Or simply, tap **Format > Style**.
- **Adjust the colors**: While working on the document, press **Format**, then choose **Show Colors**. Or, choose **Format**, tap **Font**, and then **Show Colors**.
- **Enter characters**: You may input several character sets, including those with accent marks and diacritical markings.
- **Check spellings**: As you type, the majority of applications will verify your spelling and rectify any errors automatically. These functionalities can be disabled or different options can be used.
- **See definitions**: Inside the document, choose the text you wish to know their meaning, then Control-click it, and select the **Look Up** option.
- **Text translation**: Inside the document, choose the text you wish to translate, then Control-click it, and then press the **Translate** button.

Save documents

Most applications you'll be working with will automatically save your files while you're working on them. A file can be saved at any moment.

- **Save a document**: Inside the document, tap the **File** button, then hit **Save**, type in the name, select the location to save the document (press the Options button $\vee$ to see more locations), and then choose **Save**.
- Save a document by renaming it: Inside the document, press **File**, then choose **Save As**, type in the updated name. If the **Save As** option doesn't appear, long-tap the **Option** key, and then open the **File** menu once more.

- Save as a duplicate: Inside the document, tap **File**, then select the **Duplicate** or **File** menu, and then choose **Save As.**

USE DESKTOP STACKS

By turning on Stacks, the documents on your desktop will be arranged into groups. Once you save a file to the desktop, it will automatically be put inside the applicable stack.

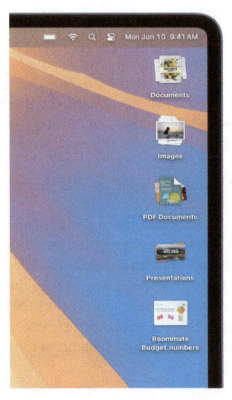

Enable desktop stacks

Tap the desktop, hit the **View** button, and then select **Use Stacks**. Or, hit Control-Command-0 on the keyboard.

Another way to enable Stacks is to Control-click the desktop, and then tap **Use Stacks**.

Browse files in a desktop stack

Place your two fingers on the device trackpad, then swipe right or left on the stack.

Expand or minimize a desktop stack

Make a stack bigger: Tap the stack on your desktop. Once it expands, double-tap an item to open it.

Minimize a stack: Tap the stack's Down Arrow icon.

Adjust how desktop stacks are grouped

You can change how the stacks are grouped or sorted.

- Tap the desktop, then select **View**.
- Next, choose **Group Stacks By**.
- Finally, select an option.
- Another way is to Control-tap the desktop, then select **Group Stacks By**, and finally, select an option.

Adjust the layout of desktop stacks

You can adjust things such as icon size, space and other details about the stack.

- Tap the desktop, then select **View**.
- Next, choose **Show View Options**.
- Finally, tap to adjust the options.
- Another way is to Control-tap the desktop, and select **Show View Options**, finally, tap to adjust options.

MANAGE FILES IN FOLDERS

Your files, images, videos, applications, audios are arranged in folders. While creating documents or installing applications and other things, you can make a folder for them so that your items are organized on your Mac.

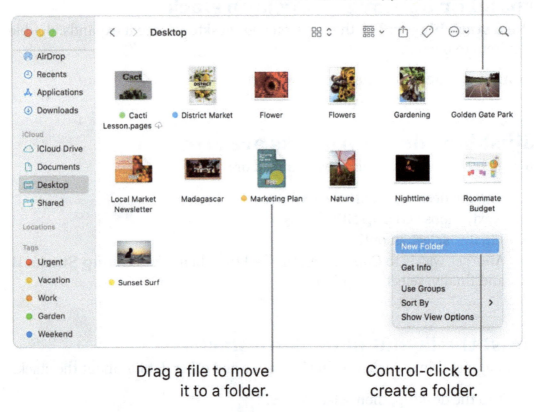

Hold the Option key and drag a file to add a copy to a folder.

Drag a file to move it to a folder.

Control-click to create a folder.

Create a folder

- First, open Finder by clicking the Finder icon ![Finder icon] from the Dock menu. Then, go to the location where you wish to create the directory. If you prefer to create it on the desktop, then tap on the desktop.
- Select the **File** menu, then tap **New Folder**. Or hit the Shift-Command-N keys.
- No new folders can be created in the current spot if the **New Folder** button is dimmed.
- Type in the folder's name, then hit **Return**.

Move items into folders

1. Select the Finder button ![Finder icon] from the Dock.
2. In the Finder menu, perform any of these actions:

- **Add an item into a folder**: Use the cursor to tap and move the item into the folder.
- **Add multiple items into a folder**: Choose the files, and then drag one of them into the folder. All the chosen files will be moved into the folder.
- **Add a window's item into a folder**: Place the cursor on the left of the window's name until you see a button showing, and then slide the button into the folder.

  Also, you can long-tap the Shift key to make the button show instantly once you place the cursor in the name area. Or, move the start of the window name into the folder without having to wait for the button to show.

- **Retain an item in its original directory and add a copy into a folder**: Choose the file or item, long-tap the Option key, and then use the cursor to tap and slide the item into the folder.
- **Retain a file in its original directory and add an alias for it in a newly created folder**: Long-tap the Option and Command keys on the keyboard, and then move the item into the folder to make the alias.
- **Duplicate an item inside the same folder**: Hit Command-D, or select the File menu, and then tap Duplicate.
- **Save a copy of your files to another drive**: Click to choose the items, then drag them into the drive.
- **Move items into another drive**: Long-tap the Command key, and then tap and move the items into the drive.

Group multiple Files into a new folder

You can speedily make a folder of files right on the desktop or in the Finder menu.

- Choose all the files you wish to group together.
- Next, **Control-click** any of the chosen file, and then click the **New Folder with Selection** option.
- Type in the folder's name, and then hit **Return**.

Merge two folders with the same name

There is a way to combine two folders that have the same name but are located in different places.

Long-tap the Option key, and then move one of the directory into the location that has a folder with the same title. Choose the Merge option from the pop-up menu that show up.

You'll only see the **Merge** option if any of the directory has files that aren't included in the other directory.

If the directory has multiple versions of the same titled files, the options that you'll see are **Replace** or the **Stop**.

Combine files into a PDF on Mac

You can merge several files into a PDF; this can be done on the desktop or Finder app.

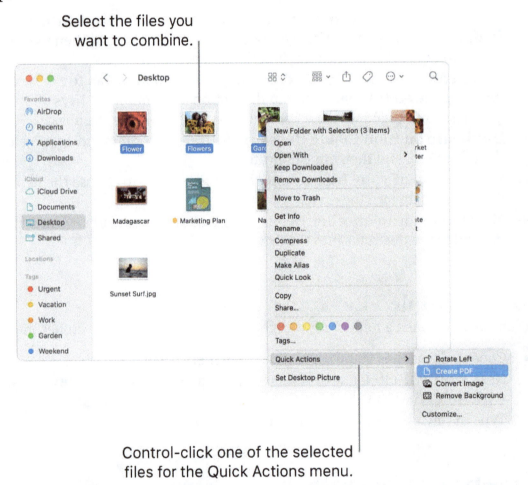

Select the files you want to combine.

Control-click one of the selected files for the Quick Actions menu.

- Select the Finder app ![Finder icon] from the Dock.
- Choose the files you wish to merge into a PDF. Or, you can choose these files from the desktop.
- The files will show in the PDF in the same sequence that you choose them.

- Next, Control-tap the chosen files, and tap the **Quick Actions** button.
- Then tap **Create PDF**.
- The will be created automatically. The file name will resemble the first file that you choose.

CHAPTER 5

BACK UP YOUR FILES USING TIME MACHINE

You can utilize Time Machine to create backups of your Mac's data, including applications, media, images, and documents, that weren't originally installed with macOS. Your Mac will automatically back up at least once an hour, once a day, or once a week once you enable Time Machine.

Even if you have disconnected your backup disc, you can still access earlier versions of your data thanks to the local snapshots saved by Time Machine. The original files and these snapshots are preserved on the same drive and are made hourly. They are saved for up to twenty-four hours or until the disk is full. Apple File System (APFS) drives are the only ones that can be used to produce local snapshots.

Time Machine can restore lost files in the event of an unintentionally deletion or update.

It is still better that you back up your files to an external hard drive, a disk on your network, or a Time Capsule, even if Time Machine produces local snapshots on PCs running APFS. With this backup, you may transfer all of your data to a different Mac in the event that your internal drive or Mac itself ever has a fault.

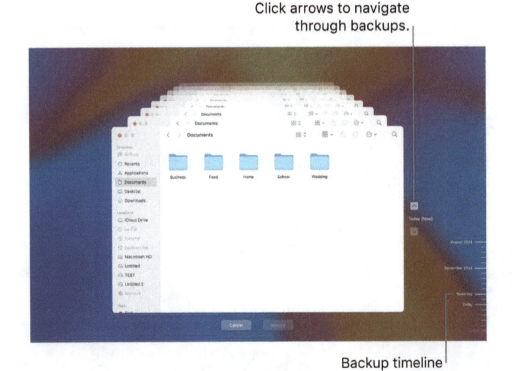

Click arrows to navigate through backups.

Backup timeline

1. Plug an external hard disk to the MacBook and power on the disk.

2. Perform any of these actions:

- **Setting up a disk in the "Time Machine can back up your Mac" pop-up menu**: If at the time of commencement, you have not configured a Time Machine backup disk, a prompt will appear asking if you wish to utilize the disk to back up the MacBook. Move the Mac's cursor to the pop-up menu that shows up, tap **Options**, then select **Set Up** to utilize this disk as a backup disk through Time Machine. (Tapping the **Close** button will make Time Machine to exit, and let the disk connect normally.)

- **Setting up a disk under the Time Machine Settings**: Press the Time Machine button 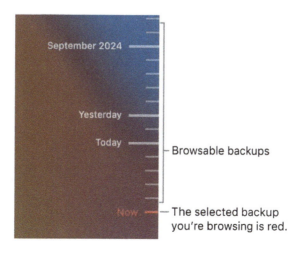 at the menu bar, and then select the **Open Time Machine Settings** option.
  If the Time Machine button doesn't appear in the menu bar, press Apple menu , then select the **System Settings** option. Hit the Control Center from the sidebar, then navigate to **Time Machine** , and finally choose the "**Show in Menu Bar**" option from the dialog window.

3. Next, tap **Add Backup Disk**. Or press the Add icon .

The option that will appear is determined if you have one or multiple backup disks that are already configured.

Restore Files backed up using Time Machine

You can simply restore deleted data or previous versions of files backed up using Time Machine.

September 2024

Yesterday

Today

— Browsable backups

Now — The selected backup you're browsing is red.

- Navigate to the window for the file you wish to restore. For instance, go to the Documents folder in order to retrieve a file that you removed from that same folder. If it's from the desktop, then you do not have to open any window.

- Go to the Launchpad app 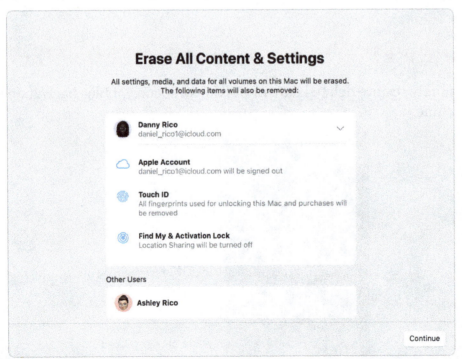 by selecting the app icon from the Dock.
- Tap the **Other** folder, then select the **Time Machine**.
- You'd be shown a notification as the MacBook connects to the backup disk.
- Utilize the arrows and timeframe to explore the local snapshots and backups.
- Choose the files, directories, or the whole disk that you wish to recover, and then hit the **Restore** button.
  The restored files will go back to its original location. For instance, if it was previously found in the Documents folder before deletion, it will return back there.

Erase your Mac

The Erase Assistant will help to restore your device to factory settings by removing all Apple services, delete downloaded apps, and sign you out of your accounts.

Ensure you've created a backup through the Time Machine before you attempt this.

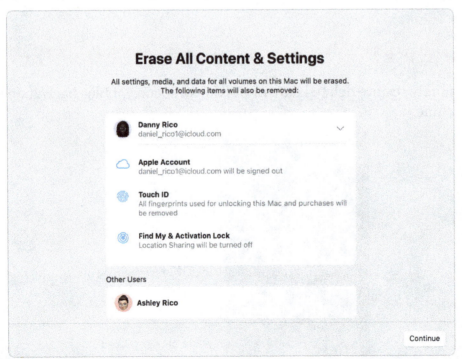

- Press the Apple menu  under the menu bar.
- Here, choose **System Settings**.

- Next, select **General** .
- Then choose **Transfer or Reset**.
- Continue by tapping the **Erase All Content and Settings** option.
- Fill in your administrator credentials, and then choose **Unlock**.
- Have another look at the items that will be removed and the settings.
- Then tap **Continue**.
- Follow the prompts.
- After the Erase Assistant finishes the deletion of the files and restores your device to factory settings, the "**Hello**" menu will appear on your monitor. You can then configure the MacBook for a new user.

Reinstall macOS

Reinstalling macOS is possible with the help of macOS Recovery, which is an integrated part of your Mac. During the reinstallation process, macOS Recovery protects all of your data and user preferences.

Reinstalling macOS requires an active internet connection.

- Press the Apple menu 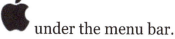 under the menu bar.
- Here, tap **Shut Down**.
- Long-tap your device power button until the machine volume and Options button is showing, then choose **Options**, tap **Continue**, and follow the prompts.
- From the Recovery menu, choose **Reinstall macOS [name]**.
- Next, tap **Continue**.
- Follow the prompts.
- Under the settings that you choose a volume, make sure to choose your current macOS volume (normally, it is the only one that's available).

Shut down or restart your Mac

You can power off or restart your MacBook whenever you like.

- Hit the Apple menu  under the menu bar.
- Then, tap **Shut Down**.

  To prevent application windows that was not closed from reopening anytime you restart the MacBook, unselect the "**Reopen windows when logging back in**" option.

  The Mac is fully powered off once the screen goes black.

  Ensure the Mac is fully powered off before you close the display.

  If the Mac suddenly stops responding, you can do a force power off. Hold down the power button until the device powers off.

  This method comes with the risk of losing unsaved changes.

Restart your Mac

- Hit the Apple menu under the menu bar.
- Then, tap **Restart**.

Start up your Mac in safe mode

Booting the Mac through safe mode can assist in detecting if the problem you are experiencing is as result of applications that opens when the device starts up.

- Hit the Apple menu under the menu bar.
- Then, tap **Shut Down**. Ensure that the Mac is powered off.
- Then long-tap the power button until you see the "**Loading startup options**" menu.
- Next, choose a volume.
- Hold down the Shift key, and choose the **Continue in Safe Mode** option.

- Your Mac will automatically restarts. Once the sign in menu shows, you will see the "**Safe Boot**" button under the menu bar.

Check if your Mac started up in safe mode

You can crosscheck if your device was really powered on in safe mode.

1. Hold down the Option key in the keyboard.

2. Next, select the Apple menu .
3. Then choose **System Information**.
4. Next, choose Software from the sidebar.
5. Under the **System Software Overview**, check what appears next to **Boot Mode**:
- **Normal**: Means your Mac isn't powered up in safe mode.
- **Safe**: Means your Mac is powered up in safe mode.

Keep your Mac up to date

From time to time, Apple updates the macOS software of the MacBook; these updates fixes some critical security issues and also updates the built-in apps.

You'll receive an alert when there's an available updates. You can choose to do it yourself or let it update automatically.

Check for updates manually

- If you're manually updating the macOS software, tap the Apple menu ,

then select the **System Settings** option, choose **General** , and finally press **Software Update**.
- If you're updating the software downloaded in the App Store, tap the Apple

menu , if available, the updates will appear next to App Store. Tap **App**

Store to carry on the installation in the App Store.

Set Mac software update options

1. Press the Apple menu .
2. Next, choose **System Settings**.
3. Tap **General**.
4. Then select **Software Update**.

5. Press the Info icon ⓘ that sits next Automatic Updates.
6. Perform any of these tasks:
- Enable the "**Download new updates when available**" option to ensure that the MacBook will download the available updates without prompting.
- Toggle on the "**Install macOS updates**" option to ensure that the MacBook will automatically install the software update.
- Enable the "**Install application updates from the App Store**" option so that the MacBook can automatically install app updates right from the App Store.
- To ensure that your device install security files, enable the "**Install Security Responses and system files**" option.
7. Then press **Done**.

   For automatic software downloads, keep your Mac's power adapter connected.

CHAPTER 6

CUSTOMIZE YOUR MAC USING SYSTEM SETTINGS

To personalize your Mac, you may adjust the system preferences. You can update the wallpaper, select a bright or dark theme, and much more.

The Mac's settings are where you'll find all of the options. Appearance settings are where you'll find options to set things like Accent color and Highlight color, for instance.

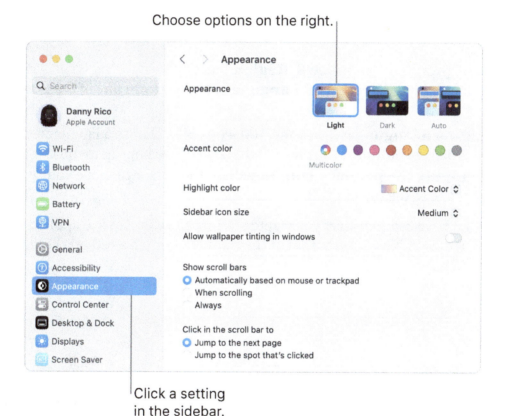

- Tap the System Settings app from the Dock. Or, select the Apple menu , then choose **System Settings**.
- Click a setting.
- The different Settings menu will show in the sidebar.
- Tap to adjust an option.

Change your Mac's language

You can change the standard language that the computer displays, which is usually the language of the nation or area where it was bought. You can change your Mac's language settings to French, for instance, if you purchased it in the US but mostly work in French.

1. Hit the Apple menu at the menu bar.
2. Next, choose **System Settings**.
3. Then select **General** .

4. Here, press the **Language & Region** button .
5. Underneath the **Preferred Languages** list, perform any of these tasks:

- **Adding a language**: Select the Add icon , choose a language, and then tap Add (the button at the lower-right edge of the pop-up menu).
- **Changing the primary language**: Use the cursor to move your preferred language to the top of the list.

  You'd be asked to restart your laptop before the changes are applied. Select the **Restart Now** (the button at the right containing a red text) to reboot the Mac.

CUSTOMIZE THE WALLPAPER

The background image of your desktop can be updated, and you can pick from the built-in images or your own captured photos.

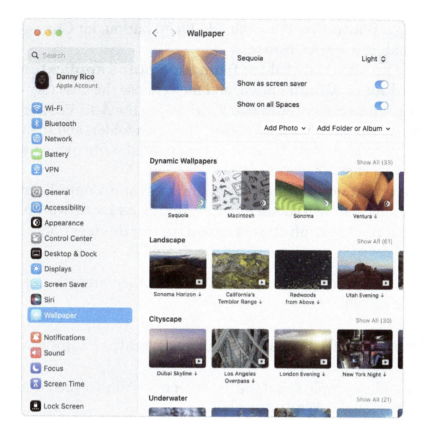

Choose a built-in wallpaper

1. Hit the Apple menu at the menu bar.
2. Next, tap **System Settings**.

- Then select **Wallpaper** .
- Navigate to any of the listed categories (Dynamic Wallpapers, Pictures, Shuffle Aerials), and then choose a wallpaper.

Add custom wallpaper

1. Select the Apple menu at the menu bar.
2. Then choose **System Settings**.

3. Next, press the **Wallpaper** button .
4. Perform any of the tasks below:
- **Adding a photograph from the Photos gallery**: Press the **Add Photo** button, select the **From Photos** option, and then choose an image.

- **Adding a photo file**: Press the Add Photo button, hit **Choose**, and choose a file, and then select **Choose**.
- **Adding an album or folder from the Photos application**: Select the **Add Folder** or **Album** option, and then choose the directory or album.
- **Adding a directory from the Finder**: Hit the **Add Folder** or **Album** option, then select **Choose Folder**, click on a folder, and then tap **Choose**.
5. There are multiple ways to select a personalized wallpaper without going to the Wallpaper settings window.
- **Utilize an internet photo**: From the Safari app, Control-click the photograph, and then choose the **Use Image as Desktop Picture** option.
- **Utilize a photograph that is saved on the device**: Choose the Finder

  app . Control-tap the photograph, and then press the **Set Desktop Picture** button.

- Utilize an image from the Photos gallery: Select the Photos icon ,

  choose a photograph, select the Share icon under the Photos menu, and then press the **Set Wallpaper** button.

Delete a custom wallpaper

1. Select the Apple menu at the menu bar.
2. Then tap **System Settings**.

- Here, choose the **Wallpaper** button .
- Place the cursor on the image, album, or directory that you wish to delete.

- Finally, press the Remove button .

If the image is currently been used as your device wallpaper, you cannot delete it.

USE A SCREEN SAVER

Screen saver provides a secure layer by hiding your desktop when you're not currently using your Mac.

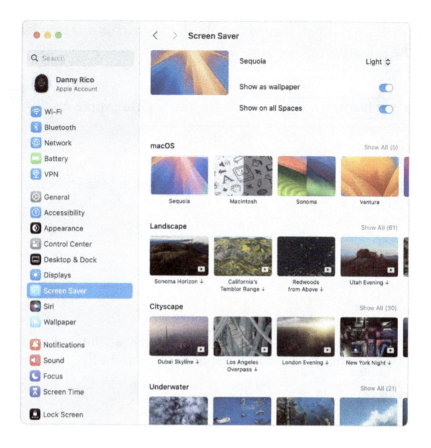

Customize the screen saver on your Mac

- Select the Apple menu at the menu bar.
- Then tap **System Settings**.

- Next, tap the **Screen Saver** button .
- Choose a screen saver from the listed categories (Shuffle Aerials, macOS, Other), and then set options for them.

Start or stop the screen saver on your Mac

Once the laptop is not in use for the duration you specify, the screen saver will begin running automatically. To adjust the maximum amount of time your Mac may be idle before the screen saver activates, do the following:

- Select the Apple menu at the menu bar, then tap **System Settings**, and finally, tap **Lock Screen** from the sidebar.

If you have hot corners turned on, place your cursor on the edge to instantly begin the screen saver.

- Or, you can begin the screen saver by tapping the Apple menu , and then selecting **Lock Screen** .

Pressing any key, dragging the mouse, or touching the trackpad will bring the desktop back into view and exit the screen saver.

CHANGE THE DISPLAY RESOLUTION

The size of items on your monitor is determined by the screen's resolution, you can manually tweak the items to appear bigger or smaller than they current are.

Set the resolution for your primary display

1. Press the Apple menu at the menu bar.
2. Next, tap **System Settings**.
3. Press the **Displays** button from the sidebar.

4. Then choose a resolution.
   - At this point, the resolution will appear in thumbnails, hover the cursor on the thumbnails to check their sizes, and then select your preferred option.
   - You can view the resolutions options in list format by Control-clicking on the thumbnail display, and then tap **Show List**. Finally, select your preferred resolution.
   - If you wish to return to thumbnail view, simply Control-tap the list view and then select the **Show Thumbnails** option.
   - If you always wish to view the resolutions in list format, tap Advanced, then toggle on the "**Show resolutions as list**" option.

Set the resolution for a connected display

If your Mac is connected to another monitor, you can set the resolution for the second display too.

- Press the Apple menu at the menu bar.
- Next, tap **System Settings**.

- Select the **Displays** button .
- Choose the display that you wish to tweak its resolution.
- Choose the resolution you wish to use.
  If available, enable the "**Show all resolutions**" option to view more resolutions for the connected monitor.

Magnify the cursor

If the cursor is too small on the screen, you can adjust its size and appearance so that it is easier to find on the display.

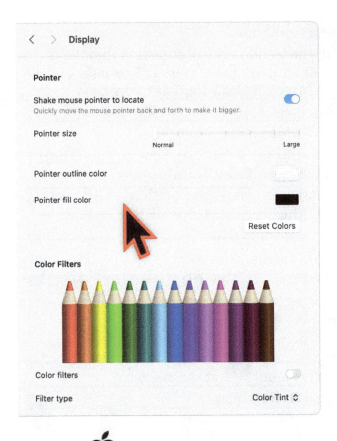

1. Press the Apple menu at the menu bar.
2. Next, choose **System Settings**.

3. Click the **Accessibility** button .
4. Next, tap the **Display** button from the right.
5. Navigate to the Pointer menu, and then set the options that appears:

- **Shake mouse pointer to locate**: Toggle on the switch so that the cursor will become bigger anytime you rapidly drag your hand on the trackpad or rapidly drag the mouse.
- **Pointer size**: Move the slider towards the "**Large**" section until it gets to your preferred size.
- **Pointer outline color**: Tap the color palette to choose your preferred color for the cursor's outline.
- **Pointer fill color**: Tap the color palette to choose a color to fill the inside of the cursor.
- **Reset Colors**: Tap this to utilize the default cursor outline color.

ZOOM IN ON MAC

To make items bigger on the Mac, you can zoom using the keyboard or trackpad.

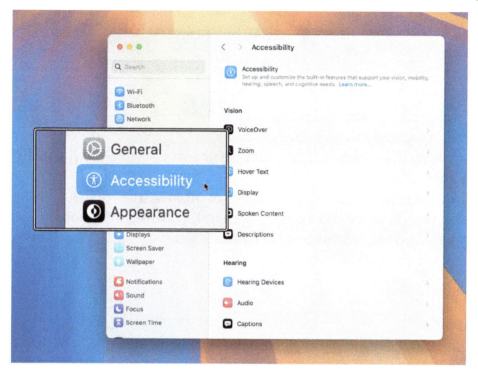

Use keyboard shortcuts to zoom

By using some keyboard combinations, you can pan the view of a menu or item.

1. Hit the Apple menu .
2. Next, choose **System Settings**.

3. Next, tap the **Accessibility** button .
4. Click the **Zoom** button.
5. Toggle on the switch next to "**Use keyboard shortcuts to zoom.**"
6. Perform any of these actions:
- **Zoom out**: Hit the Option-Command-Minus Symbol (-) on the keyboard.
- **Zoom in**: Hit the Option-Command-Equal Symbol (=) on the keyboard.
- Hit the Option-Command-8 keys to rapidly move between zoomed in and out view.

Scroll to zoom

With the combination of a specified keyboard shortcut and trackpad scrolling, you can pan the view of an item or window.

- Click the Apple menu 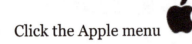.
- Then tap **System Settings**.

- Here, press the **Accessibility** button .
- Then select the **Zoom** button.
- Toggle on the switch next to the "**Use scroll gesture with modifier keys to zoom**" option.
- Next, select the "**Modifier key for scroll gesture**" dialog menu, and then select any of the modifier key (Command, Control, or Option).
- To pan the view (zoom in or out), hold down the selected modifier key, and then use the trackpad to scroll.

Tap to zoom

You can also pan the view by clicking on the trackpad.

- Click the Apple menu , and then tap **System Settings**.

- Next, choose **Accessibility** , and then click **Zoom**.
- Toggle on the switch next to "**Use trackpad gesture to zoom**."

  Perform any of these actions:

- **Rapidly move between zoomed in & out**: Tap twice on the trackpad using three fingers.
- **Slowly zoom in & out**: Click two times on the trackpad using three fingers and drag.

SEE A LARGER VERSION OF TEXT

When using Hover Text on the Mac, you may magnify the text by dragging the cursor over it. As an alternative, you can utilize Hover Typing, which enlarges the text as you write and makes it editable.

Drop off Grandma's groceries

Display a larger version of text when you move the cursor over it

When you put your cursor over text or on-screen items like application icon, Hover Text will magnify the object that's below the cursor.

- Hit the Apple menu ![Apple menu], and then choose **System Settings**.

- Tap the **Accessibility** button ![Accessibility], and then select **Hover Text**.
- Toggle on the switch next to **Hover Text**.
- Place the cursor on the text, and then long-tap the Command key to show the expanded version of the text.

See a larger version of text you're typing

Hover Typing allows you to see a zoomed in version of the text you are typing in a different window.

- Select the Apple menu ![Apple menu] from the menu bar.
- Then tap **System Settings**.

- Here, choose the **Accessibility** button .
- Next, tap **Hover Text**.
- Toggle on the switch next to **Hover Typing**.
- Once you start typing in a text field, a magnified version of the text will appear.
- Pressing the Esc (Escape) key will briefly hide the Hover Typing menu. Once you begin typing once more, the window will return.

USE HOT CORNERS

By setting up hot corners, anytime you place your cursor at a corner of the Mac, it will begin an action that you specified. For instance, moving the cursor to the upper-left edge can bring on the screen saver, or lock the display if you place it on the upper-right edge.

A default setting for the lower-right edge place is to open the Quick Note, to let you quickly take notes.

- Press the Apple menu at the menu bar.
- Then hit **System Settings**

- Next, select the **Desktop & Dock** button ⬛ .
- Here, tap **Hot Corners**.
- For the edges you wish to utilize, press the dialog menu, and then select an option, like Lock Screen, Notification Center, or Launchpad.
- Then tap **Done**.

VIEW & EDIT MOUSE OR TRACKPAD

GESTURES

Your MacBook supports a wide variety of gestures, including clicking, tapping, and pinching, which allow you to do things like quickly go to desktop, flip photographs, and zoom in on documents. Ensure you go into the Mouse or Trackpad settings to see what motions are available and to personalize them.

- Select the Apple menu  at the menu bar.
- Next, press **System Settings**.

- From the sidebar, choose the **Mouse** or **Trackpad** button.

CHAPTER 7

APPLE INTELLIGENCE

The AI technology integrated into macOS Sequoia is called Apple Intelligence. It delivers actionable insight by integrating generative models with knowledge of your unique situation. The goal of Apple's artificial intelligence (AI) is to make things easier and faster. Apple Intelligence can generate photos and spoken content and organize and summarize messages, emails, and alerts.

Use ChatGPT with Apple Intelligence on Mac

If you set up ChatGPT on the Mac, you can use it together with Siri to get answers about certain questions, request and also to generate photos and articles.

A ChatGPT account is not required, however you can link to your existing account if you choose.

Set up ChatGPT

In your first attempt of generating text or using Siri to access ChatGPT for replies, you'd be asked to enable the extension. Additionally, you can still configure ChatGPT right on the System Settings menu.

- Select the Apple menu from the menu bar.
- Then choose **System Settings**.

- Next, select **Apple Intelligence & Siri** .
- Then choose **ChatGPT**.
- Here, tap **Set Up**, and then tap **Next**.
  Perform one of these actions:
- **Utilize ChatGPT with no account**: Select the **Enable Chat GPT** option.
- **Utilize ChatGPT with an account**: Press the **Use ChatGPT with an Account** option, and then continue with the prompts.
- Be sure you're logged into your ChatGPT account if you'd like to have your inquiries stored to your conversations history.
- If in the future you choose to utilize ChatGPT using an account, tap the

  Apple menu , then click **System Settings**, hit the **Apple**

  Intelligence & Siri option, select the **ChatGPT** button, and then press **Sign In**.

Turn ChatGPT off

- Select the Apple menu from the menu bar.
- Here, press **System Settings**.

- Then hit the **Apple Intelligence & Siri** option.
- Next, tap **ChatGPT**.
- Toggle off the ChatGPT extension.

Create Genmoji with Apple Intelligence on Mac

Genmoji is the name of the personalized emoji that may be made with Apple Intelligence. Just type in your desired appearance for the Genmoji or use a photo of a loved one to make one. A Genmoji may be attached to a message, shared as a sticker or a Tapback, and many other things like that.

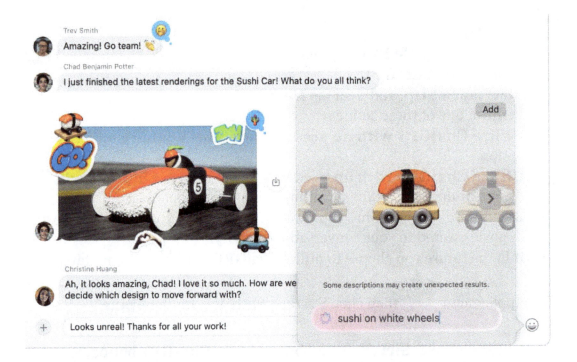

Create Genmoji

1. Once you're within an app, start to write, then hit the Fn or the globe key ⊕ + E on the keyboard. Or, if available, tap the Emoji button 😃.

    Pick one option out of these:

    - Press the Genmoji button 😃⁺ in the upper-right, type in a description on provided field, and then hit **Return**.
    - Type in some text to describe the emoji under the Describe an Emoji bar, and then select the **Create New Emoji** button.

2. Then press the Forward ❯ or Back icon ❮ to locate your preferred Genmoji.
3. Next, tap **Add**.

Refine your Genmoji

Once you've seen how your Genmoji turned out, you may tweak it by entering a new description.

For instance, if the first description was "A zebra on the moon." You can update it to "A zebra in the sparkling sky at night".

Delete Genmoji

- On the Mac's keyboard, hit the Fn or the globe + E keys.

- Then hit the Stickers icon .
- To remove a Genmoji, select it with Control-click and then select **Delete**.

Creating original photos with Image Playground

The Image Playground app utilizes Apple Intelligence to merge ideas, written explanations, and images in your picture gallery to generate customized photos in a matter of seconds.

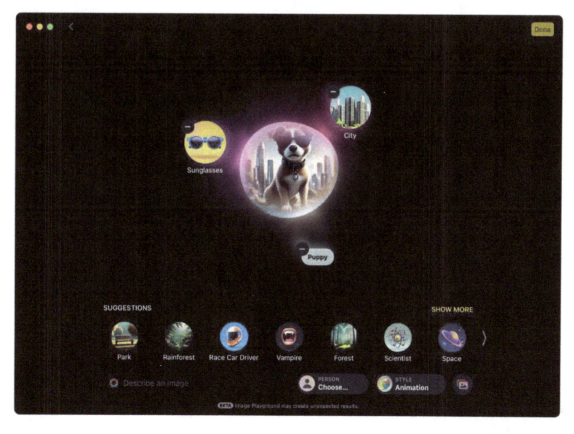

Create an image

Up to seven items can be merge to generate unique pictures.

- Select the Image Playground app .

- Next, press the Add button .
  Then perform any of these actions:
- **Generate a photo using a concept**: Tap the concept; it could be an accessory, location, theme, or suggestion.
- **Generate a photo using a description**: Press your cursor in the "**Describe an image**" bar, provide the description, and then hit the Return key.
- **Generate a photo of a person**: Select the **Person** button, and then select someone from your picture gallery.
- **Generate a photo based on a picture like food, photograph, pet**:

  Select the Photo Browser icon , and then press the **Take Photo** or **Choose Photo** button.
- **Adjust the picture style**: Select the Style option, and then tap **Illustration** or **Animation**.

- You may view different versions of a picture by pressing the Next and

  Previous buttons that are located on each side of it.
- To add a generated photo to your gallery, simply click the "**Done**" button at the upper right edge.

- To take a look at the picture in your gallery, press the Back icon .

Copy, share, or save an image

- Launch the Image Playground app .

  Perform any of these actions:

- After generating the photo, press the More icon ● ● ● , and then press the **Save**, **Copy**, or **Share** button.
- Control-tap a photo from the Image Playground library, and then hit **Copy** or **Share**.

Delete an image

- Choose the Image Playground app .
- Control-click a photo from the gallery, and then hit Delete.
- Finally, press **Delete**.

Summarize a webpage

Apple Intelligence can also summarize a webpage that you access via the Safari app.

- Select the Safari app .

- Next, select the Page Menu icon .
- Here, choose the **Show Reader** button.
- From the page's top, select **Summarize**.

- Select **Show Reader** , and then tap **Hide Reader** to go back to the default display.

Use Writing Tools with Apple Intelligence

You can utilize Apple Intelligence's Writing Tools to do things like edit your articles, generate multiple versions of a text to figure out the most suitable style and expressions, summarize what you've written, and even come up with original ideas. Anywhere you write, even on third-party applications and web pages, you can find a writing tool.

Proofread text

- Use your cursor to highlight the text you wish to refine, Control-tap the highlighted text, tap the **Writing Tools** button, and then choose **Show Writing Tools**.
- To use Writing Tools in certain applications, such as Notes and Mail, hover your cursor across the text you want to edit and then press the Writing Tool icon . Alternatively, tap the Writing Tool icon at the toolbar.
- Then, tap **Proofread**.
- The tool will check the words for spelling and grammar mistakes. A glowing line is used to highlight every updates.

    Perform one of these tasks:

- **Navigate between the revised and original text**: Select the Show Original icon from the menu.
- **Check the updates and information for each update**: Press both the Next and Previous buttons .
- **Return to the original text**: Press the **Revert** button.
- Press "**Done**" whenever you've completed the task.

Rewrite text

To make sure your assignment note or a blog article is well written, you can utilize the Writing Tools to improve it. Depending on who you're writing for and what you need it for, you may also change your writing style.

- Use the pointer to highlight the text that needs to be refined, Control-tap the highlighted text, select **Writing Tools**, and then press the **Show Writing Tools** button.
- To use Writing Tools in certain applications, such as Notes and Mail, hover your cursor over the text you want to edit and then press the button .

    Alternatively, you can tap this button at the toolbar.

Perform one of these actions:

- **Rewrite text**: Select **Rewrite**.
- **Refine the text in a specific tone**: Select the **Concise**, **Friendly**, or **Professional** option.
- **Refine the text using a description**: Hit "**Describe your change**," and then type in a description.
- The revised version of the text will appear.

Take one of these actions:

- **Rewrite over again**: Choose the **Rewrite** icon .
- **Navigate between the revised and original text**: Select Show Original icon from the menu.
- **Revert a change**: You may restore the previous edit by clicking the Undo button .
- **Go back to the original text**: Press the **Revert** button.
- Finally, tap "**Done**."

Summarize and organize text

If you wish to generate a summary for your content, then Apple Intelligence can help you.

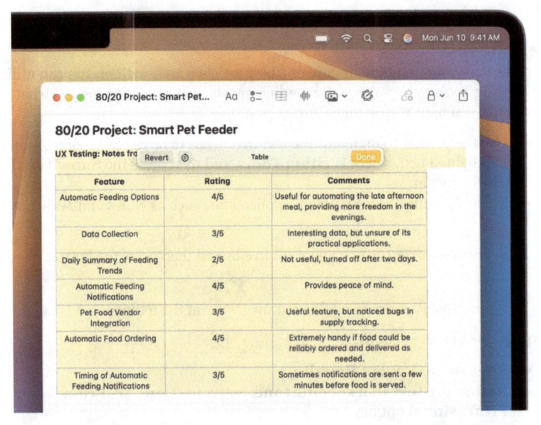

80/20 Project: Smart Pet Feeder

UX Testing: Notes fra... Revert ⟳ Table Done

Feature	Rating	Comments
Automatic Feeding Options	4/5	Useful for automating the late afternoon meal, providing more freedom in the evenings.
Data Collection	3/5	Interesting data, but unsure of its practical applications.
Daily Summary of Feeding Trends	2/5	Not useful, turned off after two days.
Automatic Feeding Notifications	4/5	Provides peace of mind.
Pet Food Vendor Integration	3/5	Useful feature, but noticed bugs in supply tracking.
Automatic Food Ordering	4/5	Extremely handy if food could be reliably ordered and delivered as needed.
Timing of Automatic Feeding Notifications	3/5	Sometimes notifications are sent a few minutes before food is served.

- Use the pointer to highlight the text that needs to be refined, Control-tap the highlighted text, select **Writing Tools**, and then press the **Show Writing Tools** button.
  To use Writing Tools in certain applications, such as Notes and Mail, hover

  your cursor over the text you want to edit and then press the button .

  Alternatively, you can press this button at the toolbar.

Use one of these methods to summarize text:

- **Summarize text**: Choose the **Summary** button.
- **Summarize the important ideas in the text**: Tap **Key Points**.
- **Arrange the unedited text in a list**: Tap the **List** button.
- **Arrange the unedited text in a table**: Tap the **Table** button.
- The revised version of the text will pop-up.

Take action after reading the summary:

- **Copy the summary**: Press the **Copy** button.
- **Insert the summary in place of the original text**: Choose the **Replace** button.

Please be aware that the Replace function will not be available if the original text is not editable.

Compose text

Toggling on the ChatGPT extension will enable you to write text using the Writing Tools.

Ensure you're no less than thirteen years old or you've attained the age of consent as dictated by your country to utilize ChatGPT.

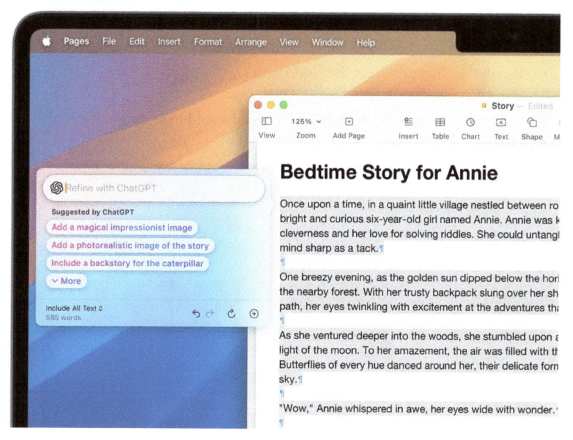

- Control-tap the file, tap the **Writing Tools** button, and then choose **Show Writing Tools**. In order to utilize Writing Tools in specific applications, such as Notes and Mail, hover your cursor over the text you want to edit and then press the button . Alternatively, you can press this button at the toolbar.
- Tap the **Compose** button.
- Type a description or plot of what you want ChatGPT to write about; it could be a fairytale story.

Do one of these things when prompted for further information:

- Enter additional information: Select the field, type in your answer, and then hit the **Send** button.
- Go ahead without providing any further information: Select "**Ignore**."

Take action after reading the text:

- **Rewrite text**: Tap the Rewrite icon .
- **Add recommendations by ChatGPT**: Choose an option, and then hit the Send button.

- **Revert a change**: Press the Undo icon .

- **Attach an image or document**: Press the Add icon .
- Finally, select **Done**.

CHAPTER 8

USE FACETIME ON MAC

You can utilize FaceTime to have video chats with loved ones or fellow employees. Like being in the same room with someone, you can see their facial expressions and emotions when you use FaceTime for video conversations. A FaceTime audio call is an alternative if you do not wish to use the camera. Your Mac's Wi-Fi is used for FaceTime calls.

Make a call

Ensure that the person you wish to call is using an Apple device.

- Select the FaceTime app  from the Mac.
- Next, select the **New FaceTime** button.
- Fill in the contact information of the person you wish to call, and then tap Return.
  You can set up a group FaceTime call by adding everyone's contact details to the "**To**" column. A maximum of thirty-two people can be added.

Take one of these actions:

- **Start a FaceTime call**: Select the FaceTime Video Call icon to initiate a video call. Alternatively, select the drop-down icon that appears next to the FaceTime Video Call icon, and then select **FaceTime Audio**.

- **Start a phone call**: Hit the drop-down icon next to the FaceTime Video Call button, and then pick the phone number that you wish to dial.

Answer a call

You can answer calls if logged in, regardless of whether FaceTime is open or not.

Perform one of these actions:

- **Answer a video call**: Press the Video icon.

- **Answer an audio call**: Press the Audio Call icon.

- **Take a video call as an audio call**: If you opt to accept as video call as an audio call, your Mac's camera will automatically go off. Press the drop-down icon next to the Video Call icon, and then tap **Answer as Audio**.

- **Receive a call while answering another call**: First, you cannot put a video call on hold. Press the Hold **& Accept** or **End & Accept** button.

Decline a call

If you receive an alert of someone calling you, take any of these actions:

- **End the call**: Choose the Decline Call icon.

- **Respond using a message or set up a callback alert**: Press the drop-down icon next to the Decline icon, and then select your preferred option.

End a call

Take the cursor to the call window, and then take one of these actions:

- **Terminate a FaceTime video call**: Hit the End Call icon .

- **Terminate a FaceTime audio call**: Press the End Call icon .

Leave a Group FaceTime call

- Press the Leave Call icon .

USE MESSAGE APP ON MAC

Once you've configured Messages, you'll be able to send personalized, group, or corporate messages with a broad range of media, including text, images, and animations.

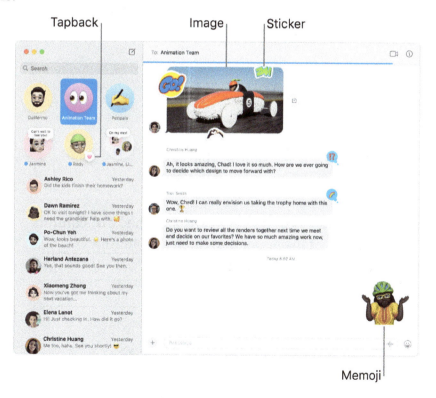

- Select the Messages app on the Mac.

- Next, press the Compose icon 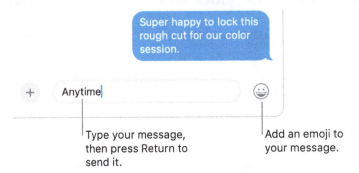 to begin a fresh message.
- Inside the "**To**" column, fill in the contact information of the recipient.
- Type your message in the text field at the window's bottom.

> Super happy to lock this rough cut for our color session.

+ | Anytime | 😃

Type your message, then press Return to send it.

Add an emoji to your message.

- Hit the **Return** key to deliver the message.

SEND AN EMAIL

You can compose, draft and send email using the Mail app. Ensure you have added an account in the app before you begin.

Send an email

- Select the Mail app on the Mac.

- Next, select the Compose Message icon.
- Fill in the email address of the recipient into the "**To**" column.
- Type in the subject of the email into Subject column.
- Enter your message into the Message column.

- Finally, select the Send button.

Save a draft

- Select the Mail app   on the Mac.
- Verify that you are in the exact message you wish to save, then select **File** from the menu bar, and then choose **Save**.

Schedule an email

- Select the Mail app   .

- Select the dropdown icon next to the Send icon ⟋ , and then select a time, or hit the **Send Later** button to choose the moment you want the email to deliver.

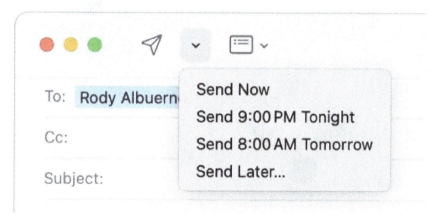

You can locate the email under the **Send Later** section from the Mail sidebar.

Dictate messages and documents on Mac

Dictation allows you to dictate text into any text field that supports typing.

Turn Dictation on or off

- Hit the Apple menu .
- Next, choose **System Settings**.

- Tap **Keyboard** .
- Navigate to the **Dictation** menu, and then toggle it on or off.
- Press the Enable button if you toggled on Dictation.

When prompted to choose how you would like Siri and Dictation get better, choose:

- **Share audio recordings**: To enable Apple to save recordings of the conversation between your Mac and Siri, press the **Share Audio Recordings**.
- **Keep audio recordings private**: Select the "**Not Now**" option.

Dictate text

- Select an application on the Mac, then tap your cursor on the location you wish to dictate the text.

- If the Microphone icon is showing, long-tap it, or tap **Edit** at the menu bar, then choose the **Start Dictation** option.

- If the microphone button shows over or under the highlighted pointer, or your Mac makes a sound to indicate that it is ready for dictation, start dictating the text.

- Even as you talk, you can continue to utilize the keyboard; you don't have to stop the dictation. As you type, the microphone button will vanish, but it returns as you stop typing.
If you need to add a punctuation mark, say the name. To begin a new paragraph, say it too.

CHAPTER 9

USE THE CAMERA ON YOUR MAC

The Mac's camera is positioned close to the top corner of the screen. Some applications like FaceTime and Photo Booth, as well other features can automatically switches on the camera. When turned on, the camera will emit a green light. After you exit any application that uses the camera, the camera will switch off.

Take a picture or record a video

You can capture one picture or collections of photos, and also shoot videos through the Mac's camera.

Choose four photos, a single photo, or a video.

Take a photo or record a video.

Apply effects.

Take a photo

- Select the Photo Booth application 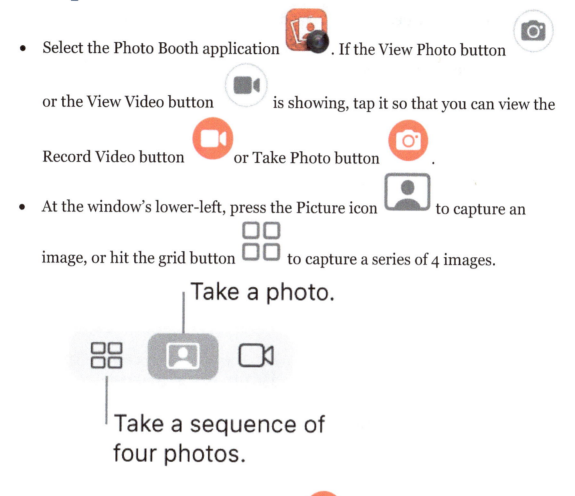. If the View Photo button

  or the View Video button is showing, tap it so that you can view the

  Record Video button or Take Photo button .

- At the window's lower-left, press the Picture icon to capture an

  image, or hit the grid button to capture a series of 4 images.

Take a photo.

Take a sequence of
four photos.

- Then press the Capture Photo button .

Record a video

- Choose the Photo Booth application . If the View Photo button

  or the View Video button is showing, select it so that you can view

  the Record Video button or Take Photo button .

- If the Record Video button ⬤ does not appear in the lower- left menu,

select the Video button ▢ .

Take a video.

- Then hit the Record Video button ⬤ .

- When you are done recording, hit the Stop button ⬤ .

Turn off the countdown or flash for photos

You can disable the countdown before the shutter captures the shot or the screen flash when you capture a picture.

- Select the Photo Booth app ⬤ .
- To deactivate the countdown, long-tap the Option key when tapping the

  Record Video button ⬤ or Take Photo button ⬤ .
- To deactivate the flash, long-tap the Shift key when tapping the Take Photo

  icon ⬤ .
- To tweak the flash setting, select Camera, and then choose **Enable Screen Flash**.
- To deactivate the countdown and flash, hold down the Option and Shift keys

  at the same time when you press the Take Photo icon ⬤ .

Take screenshots or screen recordings

- On the Mac's keyboard, hit the Shift-Command-5 keys to show the Screenshot menu.

- Then tap a tool that you wish to use to choose the object, person, or surrounding that you wish to capture or record.
- To adjust the part of the screen, move the frame to change the position or move its corners to change the dimension of the zone or section that you wish to shoot or record.
- Next, tap the **Options** dialog menu, and then select your preferred option.
- The options that will appear will depend on whether you are screen recording or capturing a screenshot.
- **Select the directory to save your file**: Beneath "**Save to,**" select any of the predefined directory or tap **Other Location** and go to the directory you prefer it to be saved.
- **Add a delay**: Under the Timer menu, select the duration before the screen capture starts.
- **Make use of a microphone when recording your screen**: Under the **Microphone** menu, choose the microphone you wish to use by placing a checkbox next to it. Choose the **None** button to disable the microphone.

Begin the screenshot or recording:

- **Full screen or parts of it**: Tap **Capture**.
- **Capture a window**: Place your cursor on the window, and then tap on it.

- **For recordings**: Tap **Record**. Hit the Stop button ⏹ at the menu bar to stop recording.

View photos & videos

You can access still images, videos, and Live Photos separately for viewing, editing, and sharing purposes. You can pan on the image or video, customize them, and even add markup.

Drag to zoom in or out.

Mark as a favorite.

Edit the photo.

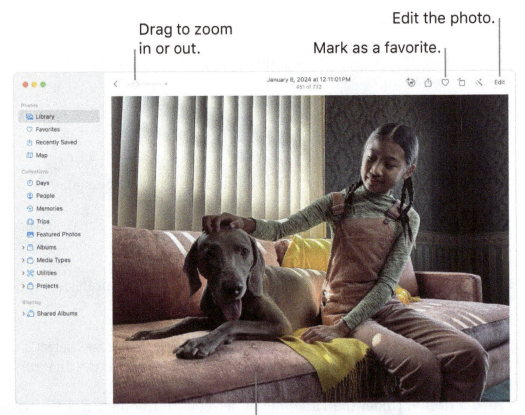

Use the arrow keys or swipe to view other photos.

View a photo

- Select the Photos app  .
- Check the sidebar, and then tap an album, Library, or a collection to view its images.
- Tap the image two times to make it appear larger in size.
- To pan the view of the image, use your cursor to move the **Zoom** slider. To move the magnified picture, just drag it.

Drag to zoom in or out.

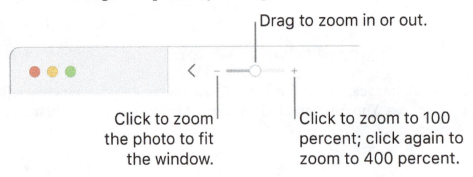

Click to zoom the photo to fit the window.

Click to zoom to 100 percent; click again to zoom to 400 percent.

- Tap the **View** button from the top, then select **Enter Full Screen** to have a picture fill the screen. Browse images by tapping the arrow keys. Hit Esc (Escape) to exit full-screen mode.

Play a Live Photo

If you shot a Live Photo using your iPhone, you can play it on the Mac. A live photo usually has a badge that sits at the top left edge.

Live Photo badge

- Select the Photos app .
- Tap two times on the Live Photo thumbnail to see it separately.

- Keep the cursor on the Live Photo mark ▶ (or the Portrait mark ƒ if it was captured in Portrait mode).

Play a video

- Select the Photos app .
- Tap the video two times to open it.
- Place the cursor on the video so that the controls button will appear.

95

- Next, hit the Play button  .

Go to the next photo or video

You can use the arrow keys to navigate between images.

Hit the arrow keys on the Mac's keyboard. Or, use your finger to swipe left or right on the trackpad.

Editing Photos on Mac

The editing features make it easy to rotate and crop your photographs and videos for better framing, among other minor adjustments. Changing the white balance, changing the exposure, can also be done on the Mac.

Click to make adjustments, apply filters, or crop and straighten photos.

Adjustment tools

Remove distractions from your images

The Clean Up tool allows you to erase unwanted items from a photo's background.

Before

- Select the Photos app .
- Tap two times on the image, tap **Edit**.
- Next, select the **Clean Up** button from the toolbar.
- Once you tap the Clean Up button, some objects in the photo will automatically highlight so that you can instantly erase them.
- Move the Size slider to choose your preferred brush size.
- Tap, markup, or circle the object you wish to erase.
- Move the Zoom slider to pan on the image, or pinch the trackpad.
- Brushing an object will blur that object.

After

- Tap the **Done** button after you finish.

Sharpen a photo or video

To make images and videos look sharper and more defined, use the Sharpen setting.

- Head over to the Mac's Photos app .
- Tap two times on the image or video, and then select **Edit** from the toolbar
- Next, select **Adjust** from the toolbar.
- Tap **Sharpen**.
- Change the sharpness by dragging the sliders for **Intensity**, **Edges**, and **Falloff** to your satisfaction.

Change definition in a photo or video

Photos and videos can have their form, midtones, and local contrast enhanced by adjusting the definition settings.

- Launch the Photos app .
- Tap twice on the image or video, and then tap **Edit** from the toolbar
- Choose the **Adjust** button from the toolbar.
- Tap **Definition**.
- Change the definition by dragging the sliders to your satisfaction.

Reduce noise in a photo or video

Pictures or videos shot in dim light could have noise in the form of grainy texture or speckles. You can minimize or remove the noise in the image or video.

- Select the Photos app .
- Double-tap the image or video, and then select **Edit** from the toolbar
- Hit the **Adjust** button from the toolbar.
- Tap **Noise Reduction**.
- Remove the noise by dragging the **Noise Reduction** slider to your satisfaction.

Apply a vignette to a photo or video on Mac

Vignettes allow you to draw attention to the middle of a picture by darkening its corners. To get the impact you like, you can tweak the vignette's size and intensity; to make it more subtle, you can soften it.

- Select the Photos app .
- Double-tap the image or video, and then choose **Edit** from the toolbar
- Press the **Adjust** button from the toolbar.
- Tap **Vignette**.
- Move the **Strength**, **Radius** and **Softness** sliders to your satisfaction.

Change white balance in Photos

You can tweak the color balance of a picture or video to fix a color cast in a part that ought to be grayscale or white. To make whites look more white, you will need to adjust the white balance to eliminate color casts.

Before white balance adjustment

After white balance adjustment

- Choose the Photos app ![Photos icon] from the menu bar.
- Tap twice on the image or video, and then hit **Edit** from the toolbar
- Choose the **Adjust** button from the toolbar.
- Next, select **White Balance**.
- Tap the dialog menu, select the white balance adjustment option that you wish to make, and then select the Eyedropper icon ![eyedropper] and select Neutral Gray, Skin Tone, or Temperature/Tint.

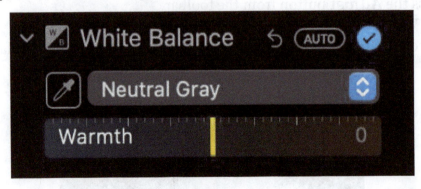

Make fine black-and-white adjustments

- Choose the Photos app from the menu bar.
- Tap twice on the image or video, and then hit **Edit** from the toolbar
- Choose the **Adjust** button from the toolbar.
- Next, select **Options** underneath **Black & White**.
- Use the cursor to drag the Intensity, Tone, Grain, or Neutrals sliders to your satisfaction.

Make fine color adjustments

When editing a video or image, you can improve the vibrance, saturation, together with the cast color.

- Choose the Photos app .
- Tap two times on the image or video, and then hit **Edit** from the toolbar
- Choose the **Adjust** button from the toolbar.
- Next, select **Options** underneath **Color**.
- Use your cursor to one of Saturation, Cast, or Vibrance slider to your satisfaction.

Create a quick slideshow

While making a slideshow, you can choose your preferred images, videos, as well as a background music and theme.

- Select the Photos app   .
- From the sidebar, select **Days** or **Library**.
- Continue by choosing your preferred images and videos, tap the **File** button, and then hit **Play Slideshow**.
- You can further customize the slideshow:

- Tap the Music button   to update the song. Hit **Browse** to view additional options.

- Select the Memory icon   to update the appearance of the slideshow.
- The slideshow will automatically store on your Mac as a memory. Select the **Memory** button from the sidebar to see it later on.

View & edit files with Quick Look

You may quickly and easily see a large preview of almost any file type without actually opening it using Quick Look. Under the Quick Look menu, you can utilize Markup, flip photographs, and crop audio and video recordings.

Rotate

Markup

Share

1. Choose one or multiple items on the MacBook, then tap the Space bar.
2. The Quick Look menu will appear. If you have made several selections, the one you last chose will be displayed first.
3. Choose one of these options from the Quick Look menu:

• **Adjust the window size**: Use the cursor to drag the window's edges. Or

   select the Full Screen icon ⊘ at the upper-left edge of the menu. To leave the full screen, take the Mac's cursor to the window's bottom area, and

   then select the Exit Full Screen icon ⤡ .

• Pan the item: To magnify the size of the photo, hit the Command-Plus (+) key, to reduce the size, tap Command-Minus (−).

• **Rotate an item**: Select the Rotate Left icon ⤹ , or long-tap the Option

   key, and then press the Rotate Right icon ⤸. Continue tapping to keep flipping the item.

- **Mark up the item**: Select the Markup icon .

- **Crop a video or audio**: Select the Trim icon , drag the yellow grip under the trim bar. Press the Play icon to see how the edits looks. Press the **Revert** button to start afresh. After making your edits, tap **Done**, then select to either create a new file or replace the existing one.

- **Go through items**: In case you've choose more than one items, tap the arrows close to the upper-left or hit the Right or Left Arrow key. Press the Play icon to see the items displayed as a slideshow when you're in full screen mode.

- **Display the items in grid format**: If you have chosen more than one item, press the Index Sheet icon , or hit the Command-Return key.

- **Open up an item**: Select the **Open with [App]** option.

- **Share item**: Press the Share icon , and then select the sharing option.

- **Copy the item's subject**: You can detach the subject of a photograph from the background by Control-clicking the photograph, then select **Copy Subject**. Paste the subject on your preferred document, note, or email.

4. After everything, hit the Space bar or press the Exit icon to exit the window.

ABOUT THE AUTHOR

Douglas C. McNally is a seasoned technology writer with a passion for making complex gadgets easy to use. With a degree in Computer Science and over 25 years of experience in the technology industry, Douglas has worked at the forefront of the tech industry, gaining deep insights into the world of smartphones, tablets, and smart devices.

Now retired from the fast-paced world of engineering, Douglas dedicates his time to writing comprehensive user guides and handbooks, helping everyday users master their devices with ease. His expertise spans iPhones, Samsung devices, Apple gadgets, Amazon products, and fitness technology, ensuring that readers stay ahead with the latest innovations.

When not writing, Douglas enjoys family life in the scenic landscapes of Alaska with his wife and two children. His mission is to empower users with knowledge, making technology accessible, practical, and enjoyable for all.

INDEX

106

107